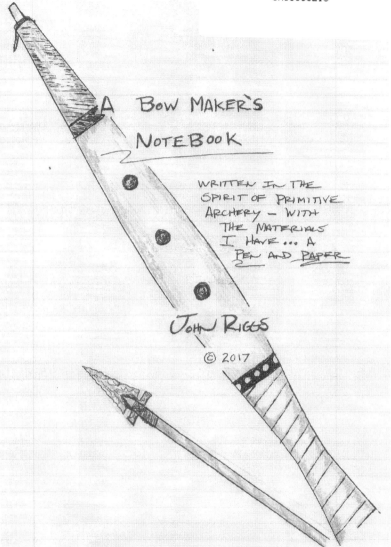

A Bow Maker's Notebook

WRITTEN IN THE SPIRIT OF PRIMITIVE ARCHERY — WITH THE MATERIALS I HAVE ... A PEN AND PAPER

John Riggs

© 2017

Dear Readers,

Greetings... Anyone who has visited any forum quickly comes to realize that any subject can be debated at each and every level. Over the years, I have come to realize that the subject of bow making is no exception: Heated arguments can develop over which bow woods are best, how backings work and differ, glues, brace heigths, english warbows, etc., etc., etc. There is a potential fight lurking in the shadows of each and every aspect of primitive archery. In many cases there is no one right or wrong because many of the tussles regard personal opinion.

I am simply writing this in the form of a personal journal. I do not intend for it to represent the "final answer" over every subject it covers. Instead, it is my version of what we all should be doing: keeping a written record of our experiences, methods, and tricks that we gather over time... This is my notebook, thank you for visiting my world.

John Riggs,
Ever Humble

TABLE OF CONTENTS

CHAPTER 5: PROJECT BOW #2 - LONGBOW

CHAPTER 6: PROJECT BOW #3 - THE GULL WING

CASE STUDY: MY PADDLE BOW   184

CHAPTER 8: THE BOWYERS FLOTE   191

THE BEGINNING

"FROM DEEP IN THE PAST, MY
COMPANION RETURNS"

THESE WORDS WERE TRANSLATED INTO OLD
NORSE, WRITTEN IN RUNES OF THE ELDER
FUTHARK, AND GRACED THE BACKS OF SEVERAL
MOLLEGABET BOWS I BUILT A WHILE BACK.
THESE WORDS DESCRIBE MY FEELINGS OF
WHAT BOWS MEAN TO US ALL : BOWS CAN
BE MACHINED FROM SPACE AGED ALLOYS AND
COVERED WITH LASER SIGHTS, SILENCERS,
DAMPENERS, AND "OTHER SHIT STUCK TO
THEM" AS I HAVE HEARD COMPOUND SHOOTERS
STATE .... OR THEY CAN BE ORGANIC
EXPRESSIONS OF OUR HUMANITY ... A CONNECTION
TO OUR NATURAL WORLD .... OUR CONNECTION
TO OURSELVES.... A GIFT FROM THE TREES,
PLANTS, ROCKS, AND OUR FELLOW CREATURES
THAT INHABIT THIS GREAT CIRCLE, GIVING US
THE STUFF FROM WHICH OUR HUNTING TOOLS
ARE MADE.

WHEN I HOLD A SINEW BACKED BOW
AND STONE TIPPED ARROWS, I TRULY FEEL
THE WORLD IN MY GRASP : ANIMAL, PLANT,
AND STONE. THEY ARE ALL REPRESENTED. IN
THIS I UNDERSTAND WHY THE LAKOTA DIDN'T

1

CALL BOWS, BOWS IN THEIR LANGUAGE, OR WEAPONS EITHER. THEIR NAMES FOR THESE SHAMANIC DEVICES MEANT GIFT OR BLESSING. WORDS DON'T ALWAYS TRANSLATE FLAWLESSLY. HOWEVER, GIFT OR BLESSING WORK. BOWS ARE NOT "THINGS", THEY TRULY ARE OUR COMPANIONS.

AND SO WE ARE HERE, MY FRIENDS.... MEMBERS OF THE TRIBE OF HUMANS JOINED IN THE PURSUIT OF CREATING THESE MYSTICAL BEINGS WHO CAPTURE OUR LIFE ENERGY AND PASS IT TO OUR ARROWS, SO THEY CAN CAPTURE THE ENERGY OF OTHER LIVING CREATURES, WHO THAN PASS IT BACK TO US, CONNECTING THE CIRCLE.

WELCOME TO THE JOURNEY

CHAPTER 1 :

THE EQUATION -

WOOD + DESIGN + EXECUTION = BOW

$$D = \sum_i^p d_i = \sum_i^p \frac{n_i}{N_i} = n_t \cdot \sum_i^p \frac{f_i}{N_i}$$

$$d_i + \delta d_i = \frac{n_i + \delta n_i}{N_i + \delta N_i} = \frac{n_i}{N_i} + \frac{\partial d_i}{\partial n_i} \cdot \delta n_i + \frac{\partial d_i}{\partial N_i} \cdot \delta N_i$$

$$\delta D = \sum_i^p \delta d_i$$

I MAKE NO CLAIM, EITHER WRITTEN NOR IMPLIED THAT I SHALL DESCRIBE ANY PIECES OR PARTS OF THIS BOW EQUATION, OR AS THE COOL PEOPLE REFER TO IT, THE BOWQUATION IN THE FOLLOWING ORDER: DESIGN + WOOD + EXECUTION = BOW.

THANK YOU FOR READING MY BOOK AND NOW THAT YOU UNDERSTAND THAT MAKING WUD BOWS IS SIMPLY TAKING WOOD AND SCRAPING INTO A BOW SHAPE, WE ARE DONE. PERHAPS THOUGH, THIS WOULD BE A GOOD TIME TO ADD THAT, THAT IS ALL YOU NEED TO KNOW TO MAKE A SLOW, WEAK BOW. BECAUSE THIS IS NOT OUR GOAL, WE MUST INSTEAD WORK ON FULLY UNDERSTANDING EACH OF THESE THREE PARTS OF OUR EQUATION SO OUR BOWS WILL BE FAST, RELIABLE, AND ELEGANT.

1) IN GENERAL, ALL BOW WOODS VARY IN THEIR PHYSICAL PROPERTIES: THEIR ABILITY TO BEND AND THEN SPRING BACK (ELASTICITY), ABILITY TO WITHSTAND COMPRESSION, ABILITY TO WITHSTAND TENSION, AND THEIR BALANCE BETWEEN COMPRESSIONAL AND TENSIONAL STRENGTH. WE CAN ALSO FACTOR IN STIFFNESS AND DENSITY.

2) THE DESIGN OF THE BOW SHOULD PUSH
THE LIMITS OF MANAGABLE STRESS AT FULL
DRAW WITHOUT CAUSING COMPLETE FAILURE
OR DAMAGE IN THE FORM OF MAJOR
STRING FOLLOW. STRING FOLLOW BEING
THAT PERMANENT BEND AN OVERSTRESSED
BOW SHOWS AFTER BEING UNSTRUNG.
YES, THE BELLY OF A BOW, ALONG WITH
THE BACK WILL COMPRESS AND
STRETCH TO SOME DEGREE, BUT IN
A PROPERLY MADE BOW WILL REACH AN
EQUALIBRIUM.

PUSHING THE LIMITS OF STRESS IN
EFFECT MEANS THAT THE MINIMUM AMOUNT
OF WOOD WAS USED, MEANING THAT THE
LIMBS CONTAIN THE MINIMUM AMOUNT OF MASS
TO MOVE, EQUATING TO THE MAXIMUM RATE
OF ACCELERATION OF THE TIPS. THIS
RESULTS IN FAST ARROWS.

3) SIMPLY STATED, THE THIRD PART OF
THE BOWQUATION IS DOING A GOOD JOB IN
EXECUTING THE DESIGN: YOUR BOW WANTS
TO LIVE. IT IS ON YOUR SIDE SO
GIVE IT EVERY POSSIBLE OPPORTUNITY TO
SUCCEED.

4

CHAPTER 2

Bow Wood

IF THE BACK FOLLOWS ONE GROWTH RING, FOLLOW THE GROWTH RING WITHOUT DAMAGING IT. LUCKILY MOST BOW WOODS CAN USE THE OUTER LAYER OF SAPWOOD FOR THE BACK: REMOVE THE BARK AND OFF YOU GO. A HANDY TIP FOR REMOVING THE THIN INNER BARK IS TO HOLD IT OVER A STEAMING TEA KETTLE AND PEEL IT OFF WITH YOUR THUMBNAIL.

IF IT IS A BIAS RINGED BOW SUCH AS A BOARD BOW, USE A BOARD WITH CLEAR STRAIGHT GRAIN.

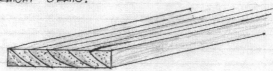

TILLER IT SLOWLY AND CAREFULLY SO THE BEND THROUGH EACH LIMB IS SMOOTH, AND MY LAST POINT IS DON'T PUSH IT. A WELL BUILT BOW WILL BREAK IF IT IS PUSHED BEYOND IT'S LIMITS: A BOW HAS A SAFE DRAW LENGTH LIMIT SO WHETHER IT IS 30 INCHES OR 23 INCHES IT IS NECESSARY TO FIGURE THAT OUT WITHOUT BREAKING IT.

THERE ARE SO MANY VARIABLES TO FACTOR IN : LENGTH OF BOW, BRACE HEIGHT, DRAW WEIGHT, WIDTH VS THICKNESS, TYPE OF WOOD, GRAIN PATTERN, BLAH BLAH BLAH, THAT TRYING TO COME UP WITH THAT EXACT POINT WHERE THE BOW GOES "BOOM" IS COMPLICATED. LUCKILY, FOR A WELL MADE SELFBOW A SAFE STARTING POINT FOLLOWS THE 20% RULE:

$$\text{DRAW LENGTH} = \frac{\text{LENGTH}}{2} - \frac{(0.2)\,\text{LENGTH}}{2}$$

FOR A SELF BOW OF 66 INCHES, NOCK TO NOCK, A REASONABLE DRAW LENGTH WOULD BE :

$$\text{DRAW LENGTH} = \frac{66''}{2} - \frac{(0.2)\,66''}{2}$$

$$\text{DRAW LENGTH} = 33'' - 6.6''$$

$$\text{DRAW LENGTH} = 26.4''$$

OF COURSE, A WELL MADE 50 POUND SELF BOW 66" LONG COULD EASILY TAKE A 28" DRAW, AND MY PADDLE BOWS WHICH ARE 64" NOCK TO NOCK AT 50 POUNDS CAN TAKE A 29" PLUS DRAW, THAT 26.4" REPRESENTS A SAFE LIMIT.

SINEW BACKED BOWS? THEY SHOULD BE ABLE TO DRAW HALF THEIR LENGTH AND RAWHIDE BEING IN THE MIDDLE.

6

WHETHER YOU MAKE BOWS FROM RAW PIECES OF TREES OR BOARDS YOU BOUGHT FROM A BIG BOX STORE, THE COMMON FACTOR IS THAT THEY WERE IN FACT ALL MADE FROM TREES. YES MY FRIENDS, BOARD BOWS ARE REAL WOODEN BOWS.

AS I WILL GO DEEPER INTO THE WORLD OF GRAIN PATTERN WHEN CHOOSING BOARDS IN THE CHAPTER ON BOARD BOWS, I SHALL NOT GO INTO THIS MATTER IN GREAT DETAIL AT THIS POINT. HOWEVER, FOR THOSE OF YOU WHO BELIEVE THAT FOLLOWING A SINGLE GROWTH RING ON THE BACK IS THE ONE TRUE ORIGINAL WAY OF THE BOW MAKER, I SHALL ONLY SAY .... WRONG!!

 BIAS RING,

 BACKWARDS,

AND DECROWNED BOWS HAVE BEEN AROUND FOR THOUSANDS OF YEARS

NATIVE PEOPLE ALONG THE WEST COAST
OF NORTH AMERICA VIOLATED GROWTH RINGS
IN FAVOR OF PRODUCING SYMETRICAL AND
HIGHLY DEVELOPED BOW SHAPES, AND BOARD
BOWS HAVE BEEN MADE FROM OAK
BARRELS AND WAGON PARTS ON THE
GREAT PLAINS LONG BEFORE THE FIRST
BIG BOX STORE OPENED IT'S DOORS.
I SHOULD ADD, THOUGH, THAT WHAT
WORKS IN ONE PLACE MAY NOT WORK
IN ANOTHER. VIOLATING RINGS IN A
HOT ARID ENVIRONMENT MAY NOT
BE AS SUCESSFUL AS VIOLATING RINGS
IN A MORE HUMID ENVIRONMENT.
THE SAME COULD ALSO BE SAID ABOUT
DIFFERENT BOW WOODS THOUGH: SOME ARE
BETTER IN HIGH HUMIDITY, OR VERY
DRY CONDITIONS.

ON A VERY PERSONAL NOTE, MY
PADDLE BOWS DEMONSTRATE HOW DESIGN
COMBINED WITH THE PHYSICAL PROPERTIES
OF RED OAK OVERCOME THE NEED TO
FOLLOW ONE GROWTH RING OR EVEN
NEEDING FLAWLESS GRAIN TO MAKE A
SELF BOW EXCEEDING 50 POUNDS AT 28"
AND BEYOND. WITH THE TYPICAL NARROW
LONGBOW, PRODUCING A RED OAK BOARD
BOW THAT DRAWS 55 POUNDS AT 28",

THAT IS ONLY 64" NOCK TO NOCK IS
NOT A SURE THING. HOWEVER, HAVING
THE LIMBS 2½" WIDE THROUGH THE
MIDLIMBS THEN TAPERING TO THE VERY
LIGHT PIN NOCKS ALLOWS THEM TO BE
RELIABLE AND FAST, WITH A 28" PLUS
DRAW. DESIGN, DESIGN, DESIGN.

"FREE YOUR MIND OF THE
SINGLE RING BIAS"

STUDYING THE PHYSICAL CHARACTERISTICS
OF WOOD, OR IN THIS DISCUSSION, COMPARING
DIFFERENT BOW WOODS CAN GET REALLY
HEAVY REALLY FAST, CAUSING HAIR PULLING
CONFUSION. IF ONE GOES TO THE WOOD DATABASE,
AN EASILY FOUND WEBSITE, FINDING THE
MODULUS OF ELASTICITY, CRUSHING STRENGTH,
HARDNESS, ETC, FOR ALMOST ANY SPECIES
IS AT HAND. THIS MAKES IT EASY TO
GET AN IDEA OF HOW MEMBERS OF A GROUP:
ROCK ELM, AMERICAN ELM, RED ELM WOULD
VARY IN DRAW WEIGHT IF THEY WERE
MADE INTO BOWS OF SIMILAR DIMENSIONS.

THIS ALSO WORKS IF ONE WANTED
TO ESTIMATE DIFFERENCES IN BOWS MADE
FROM WHITE ASH OR BLACK WALNUT, FOR
EXAMPLE, FACTORING IN THE MODULUS OF
ELASTICITY, DENSITY, JANKA HARDNESS,

PHASE OF THE MOON, THE PARTICULAR SHIMMER OF DONALD TRUMP'S HAIR THAT MORNING, ETC. REALLY HEAVY, REALLY FAST!

BECAUSE THOUGH, WE ARE ALL MEMBERS OF THE BOW CLAN WITHIN THE HUMAN TRIBE, IT IS MY SWORN DUTY TO SHARE WHAT I HAVE LEARNED AMONGST OUR CLAN.

THAT SAID, I WILL DIVIDE THE WOODS I HAVE EXPERIENCE WITH INTO GROUPS THAT SHARE SIMILARITIES AND SHARE MY IMPRESSIONS. I DO ASK YOU NOT TO USE THIS AS A BE ALL AND END ALL DESCRIPTION OF THESE WOODS. RATHER, IT IS A GOOD STARTING POINT.

"WHAT LIES BENEATH"

MOST BOW WOODS ARE PERFECTLY CONTENT TO BE MADE FROM SAPWOOD RIGHT UNDER THE BARK AS WELL AS BEING MADE FROM DEEPER WOOD. WE DO HAVE A SHORT LIST OF SPECIES THAT REQUIRE US TO WORK THE STAVE DOWN TO THE STRONGER HEART WOOD. THESE INCLUDE; OSAGE ORANGE, MULBERRY, BLACK LOCUST, AND RED ELM.

THREE OF THESE ARE PREMIUM BOW WOODS,
ONE IS NOT, AND YOU GET EXTRA
POINTS FOR GUESSING WHICH IS NOT ON
MY LIST OF FAVORITES.

OSAGE ORANGE: KING OSAGE IS A DENSE,
TOUGH PREMIUM BOW WOOD. IF THE STAVE
IS CLEAN, GOING DOWN TO A SINGLE
GROWTH RING IS EASY USING A
DULLISH DRAWKNIFE TO SPLIT AWAY THE
CRUNCHY SAPWOOD. IF THE STAVE IS
KNOTTY THOUGH, IT'S A DIFFERENT
STORY: IT CAN BE A CHALLENGE.
OSAGE HAS THE ABILITY TO WITH-
STAND GREAT AMOUNTS OF TENSION
AND COMPRESSION ALLOWING IT TO
BE MADE INTO A ROUND BELLIED
"PROPER" ENGLISH LONGBOW. IT IS
ALSO EASY TO SHAPE USING DRY
HEAT.

MULBERRY: CONSIDER MULBERRY TO BE
"OSAGE LIGHT". NOT ONLY IS MULBERRY
PHOTO REACTIVE AS IS OSAGE, THE ONLY
DIFFERENCE BEING THAT MULBERRY IS A
DEEP ORANGE IN CONTRAST TO ELECTRIC
YELLOW OSAGE. BOTH TURN DARK OVER
TIME IF EXPOSED TO LIGHT. MULBERRY
ALSO SHARES GREAT TENSILE AND
COMPRESSIONAL STRENGTH ALONG WITH

11

GREAT ELASTICITY AND A VERY CRISP
FEELING. WHY I AM CALLING IT "OSAGE
LIGHT" IS BECAUSE OF IT'S LOWER
DENSITY. ON THE SURFACE THIS MAY
SEEM LIKE A NEGATIVE BUT WHAT
IT DOES IS GIVE YOU A CHOICE: IF
YOU WISH TO BUILD A LONGBOW WITH A
DRAW WEIGHT BETWEEN 50 AND 80 POUNDS,
CHOOSE OSAGE. IF THOUGH, YOUR TARGET
WEIGHT IS 35 TO 50 POUNDS, CHOOSE
MULBERRY. DENSITY EQUALS MASS, AND
LIGHTER BOWS BENEFIT FROM LIGHTER
WOODS.

BLACK LOCUST: BLACK LOCUST CAN BE
CONSIDERED TO BE SIMILAR IN MANY WAYS
TO OSAGE, AND EVEN HAS A HIGHER
CRUSHING STRENGTH. IT IS CONSIDERED
BY MANY, ME INCLUDED AS A PREMIUM
BOW WOOD, AND WOULD BE MY CHOICE
IF I ACTUALLY GOT AROUND TO BUILDING
A BOW TO SET THE RECORD FOR WORLD'S
HEAVIEST LONGBOW. CHEROKEE PEOPLE
MADE GOOD USE OF BLACK LOCUST SO
IT WOULD BE MY CHOICE FOR A
REPRODUCTION CHEROKEE LONGBOW.
AS A SIDE NOTE, I MADE A BLACK
LOCUST LONGBOW, SNAKE SKINNED AND
SINEW BACKED FOR A VERY FAMOUS
PERSON INVOLVED IN THE MOVIE INDUSTRY.

RED ELM: ELMS ARE DIVIDED INTO HARD
ELMS AND SOFT ELMS, WITH THE HARDER
THE ELM, THE BETTER THE BOW WOOD.
RED ELM, ALSO KNOWN AS SLIPPERY ELM
IS ON THE SOFTER END OF THE SPECTRUM.
IT IS A BEAUTIFUL WOOD, AND CAN
BE MADE INTO A NICE BOW, BUT
IS IT WORTH THE EFFORT IT TAKES
TO WORK IT DOWN TO THE HEARTWOOD?

"IT'S BEGINNING TO SMELL A LOT LIKE CHRISTMAS"

JUNIPER AND YEW SHOULD BE OF NO
SURPRISE, BUT INCLUDING PINES, FIRS, AND
SPRUCES IN OUR LIST OF BOW WOODS
SURELY COULD BE. THE KEY TO USING
THE "ODD BALL" WOODS IS TO SHUN
SAPLINGS AND INSTEAD USE THE UPPER
HALF OF THE BRANCHES. THIS IS THE
IMPORT POINT: THE SPECIES IS NOT
AS IMPORTANT AS THE STRUCTURE OF THE
WOOD. LET ME EXPLAIN.... IF YOU CUT
A PINE SAPLING AND LOOK AT THE
RINGS YOU WILL SEE THAT THEY ARE
WIDELY SPACED AND THE WOOD WILL BE
WEAK AND "FOAMY". YOUNG TREES GROW
QUICKLY AND ARE UNDER NO REAL

13

PRESSURE TO DEVELOP STRONG, DENSE WOOD. AT THIS EARLY STAGE OF THEIR LIFE, THEIR MAIN JOB IS TO REACH FOR LIGHT.

INSTEAD, FIND A MATURE TREE OF THE SAME SPECIES AND CUT OFF A BRANCH. THE GROWTH RINGS OF BRANCHES WILL BE VERY FINE, WITH THE RINGS ON THE UPPER SURFACE BEING SUPER TIGHT AND THE WOOD ITSELF BEING VERY FINE AND DENSE. THIS, MY FRIENDS IS REACTION WOOD. THE WOOD "REACTED" TO CONSTANT STRESS, GROWING STRONG AND PRODUCING BOW WOOD. SOO, DO YOU THINK THAT THERE WERE HARDWOODS TO BE HAD THROUGHOUT THE ICE AGE? HECK NO, THERE WERE CONIFERS! JUST IMAGINE HOW MANY BOWS COULD HAVE BEEN GROWING ON A SINGLE SCOTS PINE TREE.

SPEAKING OF SCOTS PINE: THIS PARTICULAR CONIFER HAS EXTREMELY TOUGH WOOD. THE REAL FORM IN EUROPE IS A TALL STRAIGHT MAJESTIC TREE QUITE UNLIKE THE TWISTED STUNTED ONES FOUND THROUGHOUT THE U.S. ANCIENT EUROPEAN SCOTS PINE BOWS ARE

BELIEVED TO BE MADE FROM HEARTWOOD.
THIS CARRIES US BACK TO BIAS RINGED
BOWS, YES BOWS THAT DIDN'T FOLLOW
A GROWTH RING, THAT WERE SPLIT
FROM RELATIVELY LARGE PIECES.
WOW, BIAS RING AND SPLIT INTO
FLAT SECTIONS: THE ORIGINAL BOARD
BOW.

YEW: IT AMAZES ME HOW BOTH OSAGE
AND YEW CAN BE PERFECTLY SUITED
FOR MAKING GREAT BOWS, BUT BE
SO DIFFERENT IN ALMOST EVERY
WAY: OSAGE IS HARD, YEW IS SOFT.
IT IS SO SOFT THAT A FINGER NAIL
CAN MAKE A DENT. HENCE, HORN
NOCKS. OSAGE IS DENSE AND HEAVY,
WHILE YEW IS LIGHT. THE SAPWOOD OF
OSAGE IS JUNK, WHILE YEW'S SAPWOOD
IS BRILLIANT IN TENSION. THOUGH
OPPOSITE IN ALMOST EVERY WAY, THEY
ARE ABOUT THE ONLY BOW WOODS TRULY
ABOUT TO BE MADE INTO HEAVY
"ROUND BELLIED" ENGLISH LONGBOWS
THAT ARE SELF BOWS. IT SHOULD BE
NOTED THAT WORKING WITH YEW IS
TOXIC, SO INVEST IN A GOOD BREATHER.

15

JUNIPER: MY TAKE ON JUNIPER IS THAT
IT IS A NATURAL FOR SINEW BACKING.
IT IS A BEAUTIFUL SPRINGY WOOD AND
WITH A LAYER OF SINEW ON THE BACK
SUPPLYING TENSIONAL STRENGTH, IT IS
IN MANY WAYS AS GOOD AS A WOODEN
BOW CAN GET. THOUGH I HAVE HEARD
THAT IT'S REAL SPRING IS IN THE
SAPWOOD, I USE BOTH THE SAPWOOD AND
THE HEARTWOOD WITH GREAT RESULTS.
THEORETICALLY ONE COULD MAKE A
BOW VISUALLY SIMILAR TO A YEW LONG-
BOW USING A THIN LAYER OF LIGHT
COLORED SAPWOOD FOR THE BACK AND
THE DARKER HEARTWOOD FOR THE
BELLY. JUST KEEP IN MIND THAT
THERE IS A DIFFERENCE IN COLOR
AS WELL AS BEING LIMITED IN DRAW
WEIGHT. THE MAXIMUM POSSIBLE DRAW
WEIGHT IS FAR LIGHTER THAN WHAT
YEW CAN YIELD.

ASSORTED PINES, SPRUCES, AND FIRS: ANY OF
THESE WOULD BE MY CHOICE FOR A QUICKY
SURVIVAL BOW. USING THE UPPER SURFACE
OF THE BRANCHES, THEY YIELD BOW WOOD
THAT WORKS WELL GREEN, 100% GREEN
ALONG WITH PRODUCING BOWS ABOVE 40
POUNDS THAT RESIST STRING FOLLOW.

I WOULD SUGGEST MAKING THEM ON THE
HEAVY SIDE, DEFLEXING THE TIPS AND
SHOOTING THEM AT REDUCED DRAW LENGTHS.

"A ROSE BY ANY OTHER NAME"

APPLE, SERVICE BERRY, AND DOGWOOD WHICH
IS ACTUALLY A CORNUS NOT IN THE ROSE
FAMILY AS ARE THE FIRST TWO, ARE
RESPECTABLE BOW WOODS. THOUGH I
WOULDN'T PLACE THEM AT THE TOP OF
MY LIST OF GO TO MATERIALS, THEY ARE
A GOOD SOURCE OF MATERIAL.

"THE MOUSE RAN UP THE CLOCK"

HOP HORNBEAM AND HICKORY ARE BOTH VERY
TOUGH BOW WOODS, WHICH FOR ME MEANS THAT
THEY ARE GOOD, RELIABLE CHOICES FOR
HEAVIER BOWS. ON THE POSITIVE SIDE, THE
CHANCES ARE INCREASED FOR THE BEGINNING
BOW MAKER TO PRODUCE A BOW OF HEALTHY
WEIGHT THAT WON'T MYSTERIOUSLY EXPLODE.
THEY ARE TOUGH AND HAVE GREAT STRENGTH
IN BOTH TENSION AND COMPRESSION. THE
DOWNSIDE IS POTENTIAL STRING FOLLOW,
IN THE CASE OF HICKORY BECAUSE IT'S
ABILITY TO ABSORB MOISTURE.

17

However, both are happy to receive heat treated bellies to correct that issue, along to being go to woods for native bows! Many tribes in North America used both.

"Oh Canada"

I love MAPLES! It doesn't get more clear than that. Maple has a crisp, fast feeling whether it is vine maple, hard maple (included is sugar maple), or striped maple. Striped maple has the added benefit of the thin, tough bark which serves as a good backing, ie, leave the bark on. I have the best luck making the bows a bit wider, hence thinner so the compressional strength doesn't overcome the tensile strength.

"The Wise old man of the woods"

What is reality? I bet that we have all wondered about that and as time passes and we get older that question deepens. What is out there that we can't see, or hear, and certainly can't

BEGIN TO MEASURE. BUT FROM TIME TO
TIME WE GET THESE TWINGES OF CLARITY
WHEN WE UNDERSTAND CONNECTIONS, AND
FOR ME, A KINSHIP TO _OAK_ IS ONE OF
THOSE CONNECTIONS. I AM SURE, MY
FRIENDS, OTHER WOODS SPEAK TO YOU, BUT
OAK SPEAKS TO ME.

WHEN I HOLD ONE OF MY RED OAK
PADDLE BOWS, A PERFECT COMBINATION OF
MATERIAL AND DESIGN, THEY NOT ONLY
HAVE A POSITIVE FEELING, THEY ACT
LIKE THEY HAVE MINDS OF THEIR OWN
AND WE ARE IN A PARTNERSHIP. THEY
SEEM TO BE DRAWN AND LOOSED WITHOUT
ME HAVING TO THINK ABOUT AIMING. YEP,
I LIKE OAK AND OAK LIKES ME. RED
OAK AND WHITE OAK ARE VERY RELIABLE
BOW WOODS AND WHICH ONE I CHOOSE:
RED FOR A PADDLE BOW UP TO 55
POUNDS AND WHITE OAK FOR HIGHER
WEIGHTS. THEY ARE SIMILAR IN BEHAVIOR
BUT DIFFERENT IN STIFFNESS: WHITE
IS MORE SUBSTANTIAL.

"WAKE UP!!"

HIDDEN AMONGST THE CLAMMER
OF OSAGE, YEW, AND HICKORY, ARE

TWO SLEEPERS THAT BARELY GET ANY ATTENTION AT THE "BOW WOOD PROM". WHILE EVERYONE IS WATCHING THE COOL WOODS DANCE AND WAITING TO SEE WHICH POPULAR WOODS WILL BE VOTED PROM KING AND QUEEN, THESE TWO WOODS ARE SPIKING THE PUNCH: WALNUT AND CHERRY.

WALNUT IS A WONDERFUL BOW WOOD BOTH IN SAPWOOD AND HEARTWOOD. I DO PREFER THE REDS AND CHOCOLATES OF IT'S HEARTWOOD FOR NO OTHER REASON THAN IT'S BANDED BEAUTY. WALNUT HAS AN ALMOST PLASTIC FEELING WITH A GOOD BALANCE OF COMPRESSION AND TENSIONAL STRENGTH. THIS FINE WOOD IS AS SUITED FOR SELFBOWS AS IT IS SINEW BACKED.

CHERRY IS ANOTHER SLEEPER: LIGHT, BEAUTIFUL, AND SPRINGY. IT CAN CERTAINLY BE MADE INTO A SELFBOW, BUT I WOULD SINEW BACK IT TO MAKE BETTER US OF IT'S ELASTIC PROPERTIES AND COMPRESSIONAL STRENGTH. AS WITH THE MAPLES, CHERRY IS PRONE TO HAVING IT'S COMPRESSIONAL ABILITIES OVERTAKE IT'S ABILITY TO WITHSTAND

TENSION. WHERE AS HICKORY IS TENSION
STRONG, AND WOODS SUCH AS OAK ARE
BALANCED, CHERRY FAVORS COMPRESSION
AND ELASTICITY. PLEASE DON'T LET
THIS STOP YOU FROM BUILDING A CHERRY
SELFBOW AS IT IS POSSIBLE GOING
WIDER AND THINNER, DO THOUGH TAKE
ADVANTAGE OF IT STREGTHS AND SINEW
BACK THIS GREAT WOOD.

"BIRDS OF A FEATHER"

IF YOU HAVE WORKED WITH ELM YOU
WILL UNDERSTAND MY QUOTE: THE ELMS
HAVE INTERLOCKING GRAIN WHICH WHEN
FINISHED, THEIR SMOOTH SURFACES GIVE
THEM A FEATHERY APPEARANCE. THIS
INTERLOCKING GRAIN IS WHY THEY ARE
NOT ONLY DIFFICULT TO SPLIT, THEY ARE
TOUGH IN TENSION. ONE WOULD HAVE TO
MAKE SERIES MISTAKES IN EITHER DESIGN
OR EXECUTION TO HAVE AN ELM BOW
EXPLODE. EVEN VIOLATING GROWTH RINGS
ON THE BACK (WITHIN LIMITS) POSES LESS
OF A PROBLEM THEN IN OTHER WOODS
AS THIS INTERLOCKING GRAIN HOLDS THEM
TOGETHER. ELMS COME IN PLEASING COLORS,
AMERICAN ELM BEING YELLOW AND RED ELM,
RED. THE MAKE HANDSOME BOWS.

21

OF ALL THE WOODS I HAVE WORKED WITH, ELM IS THE MOST PRONE TO TWISTING AND BECOMING UNUSABLE IF THE STAVES ARE SPLIT AND LEFT TO DRY ON THEIR OWN. I SUGGEST DOING ONE OF TWO THINGS IF YOU CUT YOUR OWN ELM.

1) CUT THE LOGS INTO BOW LENGTH SECTIONS, GIVING YOURSELF A LITTE EXTRA LENGTH AS A SAFETY MARGIN FOR END CHECKING, ETC. THEN, SIMPLY CUT LENGTHWISE, END TO END, DOWN TO THE LOG'S CENTER WITH A CHAINSAW, REMOVE THE BARK, PAINT THE ENDS WITH GLUE OR LATEX PAINT, AND FORGET ABOUT IT (THEM) IN A COOL DRY PLACE FOR A YEAR.

2) YOUR OTHER OPTION IS TO REDUCE EVERY POSSIBLE BOW YOU CAN SQEAK OUT OF YOUR LOGS INTO GREEN FLOOR TILLERED BOWS AND LASH THEM TO BOARDS EITHER FLAT, OR BLOCK THEM UP TO SHAPE THEM INTO GULL WINGS, RECURVES, ETC.

22

ELM BOWS HAVE AN ALMOST MYSTICAL REPUTATION GIVEN THEIR HISTORY: MOLLEGABET, HOLMGAARDS, WELSH LONGBOWS, SO IT IS WORTH MORE THAN A SECOND LOOK. DO KEEP IN MIND THAT ALL EMS ARE NOT ALIKE AS THEY RUN THROUGH A SPECTRUM OF DENSITY AND STIFFNESS. THERE ARE HARD ELMS AND SOFT ELMS WITH ROCK ELM BEING ON THE HARD END, RED AND AMERICAN ON THE SOFTER END AND THE MYSTICAL WYCH ELM FALLING IN BETWEEN. WE ALL NEED MORE MYSTICAL IN OUR LIVES, ME INCLUDED, SO IF YOU KNOW WHERE I CAN SCORE A WYCH ELM STAVE PLEASE LET ME KNOW!!

"GOING BUT NOT FORGOTTEN"

IF I WAS TO DEDICATE THIS BOOK TO A WOOD, IT WOULD BE DEDICATED TO WHITE ASH. NOT SO MUCH BECAUSE I CONSIDER IT TO BE THE BEST OR MOST NOTABLE BOW WOOD. IT IS NOT. WHITE ASH IS A VERY GOOD AND RELIABLE BOW WOOD, BUT IT ISN'T THE BEST. I WOULD DEDICATE THIS BOOK TO WHITE ASH BECAUSE IT IS DISAPPEARING DUE

To attack from the emerald ash borer, a Chinese invader that landed in Detroit hidden in shipping material. Sadly we are losing all of our ash's; pumpkin ash which may already be gone, black ash which is known for native black ash baskets, and white ash which is known for many things besides bows and arrow shafts.

White ash is reliable. It is also easy to split, balanced in tension and compression, and an authentic wood choice for tribal bows. It is easy to shape by steaming and boiling, and benefits from heat treating the belly.

It is a great loss to witness the decline of this fine family of woods who have given us so much.

"Conscientious Objector"

I don't cut birch trees. I have made birch bows but I've given up my birch cutting ways.

24

CHAPTER 3:

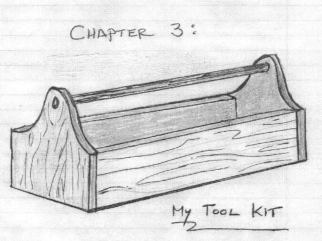

My Tool Kit

OVER THE YEARS, THERE HAS BEEN
AN EBB AND FLOW OF WHAT I WOULD
CONSIDER TO BE MY FAVORITE TOOLS. I
HAVE, AS MANY BEFORE ME, CREATED
BOWS WITH ONLY A KNIFE. NOW, AFTER
MANY YEARS OF TRIAL AND SUCCESS MY
TOOL KIT HAS EVOLVED INTO A
SIMPLE GROUP OF TOOLS THAT SERVE
ME WELL. MOST IF NOT ALL OF
THESE WILL BE FAMILIAR TO YOU
WHICH WILL MAKE THIS AN EASY
CHAPTER TO WRITE.

MY SHAVING BENCH:

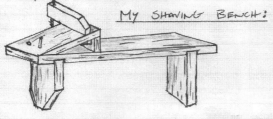

I MAY HAVE A FAVORITE WOOD
SHAPING TOOL FOR EACH PART OF THE
PROCESS, BUT I COULD ALWAYS USE
SOME OTHER TOOL TO DO THE SAME
JOB. I HAVE NO REALLY GOOD ALTERNATIVE
TO SECURE MY WORK PIECE AS WELL AS
MY SHAVING BENCH. A JORGANSON CLAMP
HOLDS THE BOW SECURELY ALLOWING ME
TO MOVE AROUND MY WORK AND WORK
FROM ANGLES I WOULD BE UNABLE TO

REACH IF I USED A "DUMBHEAD BENCH".
I HAVE TWO HOLES AT THE BASE OF
THE SOFT, CEDAR "RAMP" THAT CAN
HOLD PINS I'VE MADE FROM OSAGE
SCRAP: WHEN THE BOW IS CLAMPED
AND RESTING AGAINST A PIN, IT
CAN NOT ROTATE BECAUSE OF SIDE
PRESSURE. YOU COULD OF COURSE HOLD
THE BOW IN YOUR HANDS, USE A
PADDED VICE, OR TIE IT TO A FENCE
RAIL, BUT HAVING A GOOD BENCH
IS A GOOD THING.

FERRIERS RASP:

THIS IS MY SHAPING
WORKHORSE, PERIOD!

SOME FAVOR DRAWKNIFING,
I FAVOR RASPING, AND THIS
ONE WORKS FAST EVEN ON
ROCK HARD OSAGE. IT MAY SEEM LIKE
THAT WIDE, FLAT SURFACE CAN'T WORK
AROUND INSIDE CURVES OR IT WOULD LEAVE
A DEEPLY SCARRED SURFACE BUT WITH
PROPER TECHNIQUE, THOSE ROUGH TEETH
CAN WORK WITH FINESSE.
   * ALL FERRIERS RASPS WERE NOT
CREATED EQUAL! SPEND A LITTLE MORE

26

ON A HIGH CARBON STEEL RASP MADE
IN ITALY.... VIVA ITALIA!!

SANDING BLOCKS AND SANDPAPER:

SOME BOW MAKERS GRAVITATE TOWARDS
DRAWKNIVES AND SCRAPERS. OTHERS
FAVOR RASPS AND SANDING. I HAVE DONE
BOTH BUT DEFINITELY FAVOR RASPING
AND SANDING.

* TANGENT ALERT *
  DO AN IMAGE SEARCH FOR
  THE FUL COMPANY OF
  . LOOK FOR THE
  PICTURE OF THEIR COAT OF
  ARMS WHICH WAS GRANTED
  TO THEM IN 1488. THE
  THREE OBJECTS IN THE
  ARMS ARE ALL BOWYERS
  FLOTES..... 'NUFF SAID....

MY THREE SANDING BLOCKS:

WOOD...

FOAMY SANDING BLOCK......

ROUND THING

27

ARE....... A BLOCK OF WOOD THAT
FITS AN EIGHTH SHEET OF SANPAPER,
A SLIGHTLY LARGER FOAMY SANDING
BLOCK THAT IS ACTUALLY A SANDING
BLOCK. BEING FOAMY ALLOWS IT TO
WORK AROUND CONTOURS. I USE THE
SAME EIGHTH SHEET OF SANPAPER
BUT I HOLD IT ON THE BLOCK
SIDEWAYS. THE "ROUND THING" IS
EITHER AN EMPTY ROLL OF B50
WITH THE FLANGE REMOVED OR A
BOTTLE OF ACRYLIC ARTIST PAINT.
THEY BOTH WORK IN AREAS SUCH
AS HANDLES.

My "BIG BOY" SANDING BLOCK
WAS MADE FROM 2, 3/4" X 2" BOARDS
WHICH FORM A "T":

WITH STRIPS OF 80 GRIT
GLUED TO THE UPPER BOARD. WITH SUCH
A LONG AREA, THE SANDPAPER LASTS A
GOOD LONG TIME AND ALLOWS ME TO WORK
LONG AREAS DEAD FLAT. IT'S ALSO GREAT
FOR WORKING ARROW SHAFTS.

THE SCRIBOMATIC:

SPLIT ALLOWS FOR TIGHT FIT

NOTCH RIDES ALONG BACK OF BOW

RUBBER BAND SUPPLIES PRESSURE TO FRICTION BLOCK

I ENCOURAGE EVERYONE TO MAKE SOME FORM OF SCRIBING TOOL. IN MY EARLY DAYS I WOULD CUT A STRIP OF CEREAL BOX AND "RIDE IT" ALONG THE LENGTH OF LIMBS TO MARK THICKNESS, BUT THIS DEVICE TOOK SUCH LITTLE TIME TO MAKE AND WORKS SO WELL, IT HAS BECOME ONE OF MY FAVORITE TOOLS.

The Support Staff:

Less flashy but still important are; a 48" metal straight edge, string for finding and marking center lines, a fine point sharpy, pencils (never enough pencils), and poster board for making templates.

Tillering Stick & Tillering String:

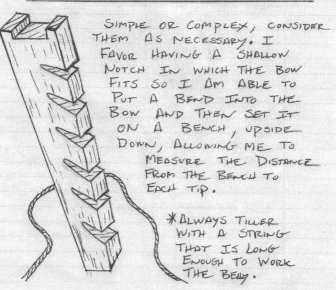

Simple or complex, consider them as necessary. I favor having a shallow notch in which the bow fits so I am able to put a bend into the bow and then set it on a bench, upside down, allowing me to measure the distance from the bench to each tip.

* Always tiller with a string that is long enough to work the belly.

SCRAPERS:

I HAVE THREE SCRAPERS: A
WESTERN CUTLERY W84 KNIFE THAT
IS THE SAME KNIFE I USED FOR
MY FIRST BOW. IT IS A BASIC
FULL TANG KNIFE THAT IS ABLE
TO WORK DIPS AND VALLEYS, ALONG
WITH WORKING AROUND KNOTS IN
OSAGE AND MULBERRY.

FOR WORKING FLAT BELLIES, SMOOTHING
AFTER RASPING OR TILLERING, I
HAVE WHAT I BELIEVE IS CALLED
A SWEDISH KNIFE. IT RESEMBLES
A SMALL DRAWKNIFE WITH STRAIGHT
HANDLES.

I ALSO USE A DRAWKNIFE
AS A SCRAPING TOOL.

ASSORTED STUFF:

3/16" ROUND RASP FOR STRING GROOVES,
A BASIC 4 SURFACE NICHOLSON RASP
FOR FINE WORK, WEDGES AND HAMMER
FOR STAVE SPLITTING, MY GREAT
QUALITY SILKY HANDSAWS, AND A
SHARP HATCHET. I ACTUALLY REGROUND
MY HATCHET SO IT IS ONLY BEVELED
ON THE SIDE THAT FACES AWAY
FROM THE WOOD WHEN I CHOP AT
A STAVE. HAVING A "BROADAXE" STYLE
BEVEL ALLOWS IT TO DIG IN AT
SHALLOW ANGLES. UNLIKE MY DRAW
KNIFE, I KEEP MY HATCHET VERY
SHARP.

THE DRAWKNIFE:

My DRAWKNIFE GETS USED FOR
SUCH TASKS AS PEELING LOGS AND
WORKING OSAGE, MUBERRY, OR BLACK LOCUST
DOWN TO THE HEARTWOOD. UNLIKE MY KNIVES,
MY DRAWKNIFE IS RELATIVELY DULL; DULLER
ON ONE SIDE AND BARELY SHARP ON THE
OTHER. I FIND THAT WORKING MY WAY

32

Through the sapwood of Osage and Mulberry is more of a splitting process rather than deftly slicing with a razor sharp blade.

My advice for working Black Locust down to the heartwood through the tough pin knots and tough sapwood is... kind of tough, so wait until you have enough experience to not require my advice. Ironic, isn't it?

Power Tools:

Along with my hand tools, I do use power tools. My favorites are my orbital disk sander and Bosch jigsaw. Building your tool kit can begin and end at a hatchet and knife but it doesn't have to. I do believe that bow makers should be able to craft bows simply, so every so often I will go into the woods and make a bow.... simply. I call it, "Maintaining My Skillages".

I HAVE ALWAYS SEEMED TO HAVE AN
ABILITY TO GET INTO THE MINDS OF DEER
AND ANTICIPATE THEIR MOVEMENTS.

IT HELPS IN TRACKING WHERE THE ONLY
SIGN MAY BE RANDOM DROPS OF BLOOD OR
GETTING IN FRONT OF THEM FOR AN AMBUSH.
ONE TIME I HAD A PARTICULAR DEER THAT
I WANTED TO AMBUSH SO I TRAILED HER
THROUGH THE WOODS FOR SOME DISTANCE
BEFORE CIRCLING AROUND AND SETTING UP
NEAR A GULLY. THE GULLY OVERLOOKED
A TRAIL THAT I THOUGHT SHE WOULD
MOVE ALONG. IT WAS A PERFECT SPOT
TO WAIT AS SHE WOULD BE BLIND TO
ME WHEN SHE CAME DOWN A SHORT
STEEP RISE. HER PATH WOULD FORCE HER
TO BE LOOKING AWAY FROM ME WHERE
I WAS SITTING ABOUT 15 YARDS AWAY.

IT WAS PERFECT, PERFECT EXCEPT
SHE DIDN'T COME DOWN THAT PATH WHEN
I EXPECTED HER TO, SO I CONTINUED
TO WAIT.... UNTIL I HEARD SOMETHING
DIRECTLY BEHIND ME.

I SLOWLY TURNED, ONLY TO SEE
HER STANDING ONLY A MATTER OF A FEW
FEET BEHIND ME, JUST WATCHING ME.

34

NATURALLY, I PUT MY BOW DOWN AND DID
THE ONLY THING I COULD HAVE DONE AT
THE TIME: I MADE "MOOSE ANTLERS"
WITH MY THUMBS IN MY EARS AND STUCK
MY TONGUE OUT..... SEEMED LIKE THE
THING TO DO AT THE TIME, BECAUSE
SHE OUTSMARTED ME WITH STYLE.

THERE WAS NO REAL TIME FOR ME TO
TURN AND TAKE A SHOT BECAUSE SHE WOULD
HAVE TURNED AND RUN. MORE IMPORTANTLY
SHE GAVE ME A REALLY GOOD LAUGH AND
IN HER WAY, WANDERED OVER TO SAY
"HI".

DEER MEAT DEFINITELY HELPED ME
MAKE IT THROUGH THE LEAN TIMES.
FUNNY THOUGH, IT IS THE STORIES LIKE
THIS THAT I REMEMBER SO FONDLY.

CHAPTER 4

PROJECT
BOW #1
"THE D BOW"

A SIMPLE WOODEN
SPRING

Preface:

In my position as the resident manager of a nature preserve, or a I refer to myself jokingly, the king of Swiftsylvania, I develop childrens' programs which include crafts.

Some years ago, a particular craft project was creating a mouth bow: a simple musical instrument which is no more than a small bow held against the teeth and the string plucked.

Within an hour before the program was to begin I looked out of the window from my office in the nature center... My daughter and another employee were playing "Robin Hood" with their mouth bows, shooting stick arrows over a tall spruce tree next to the drive. To me, it was a clear message to come up with another, non-weapon based project on the fly.

However, to someone thousands of years ago in a totally different reality, who may have spotted their daughter shooting sticks with a mouth bow... it could have been a life changing event.

36

I AM NOT SAYING THAT THIS IS HOW THE
FIRST BOW AND ARROW ENTERED OUR LIVES,
IT IS MORE DIRECTED TOWARD HOW IT
FELT TO DISCOVER THIS GIFT AS THE
LAKOTA REFERRED TO IT .... A DEVICE
THAT WOULD FOREVER WEAVE IN AND OUT
THROUGH OUR EXISTANCE : ENTER THE
BIRTH OF THE BOW AND ARROW.

YOU MAY BE LIKE ME, FULLY ABLE TO
BUILD BOWS BUT STILL ENJOY READING BOOKS
ON THE SUBJECT FOR FUN AND REFERENCE.
POSSIBLY PICKING UP HANDY TIPS FROM
OTHER VIEWPOINTS.

HOWEVER, IF YOU HAVE JUST BEGUN
YOUR JOURNEY, IT IS MY RESPONSIBILITY
TO HELP YOU DEVELOP KNOWLEDGE AND SKILLS
DURING THIS PHASE OF YOUR LIFE. THIS
IS HOW I DECIDED UPON THE FOLLOWING
THREE PROJECT BOWS. EACH OF THE
THREE BOWS ARE SIMILAR, AS THEY ARE
ALL BOWS, BUT THEY HAVE DIFFERENCES
WHICH AS A GROUP WILL GIVE YOU A WIDE
VARIETY OF SKILLS AND TECHNIQUES. IN
ADDITION TO STEP BY STEP DIRECTIONS,
BOW THEORY WILL BE MIXED IN GIVING YOU
UNDERSTANDING.

You Shall Be Visited By Three Bows This Night: The First At The Stroke Of Midnight..., Poor Impulse Control, Let Me Start Over.... The Three Project Bows Include A Simple, Unbacked "D" Bow, A Rawhide Backed "American Style" Longbow, Made From A Red Oak Board, And A Northern Plains Style Horse Bow That Is Sinew Backed — The Gull Wing. If These Descriptions Of Our Project Bows In Any Way Leave You With More Questions Than Answers, Never Fear, Soon Everything Will Become Clear.

"D Is For Bow"

Welcome To The Actual Bow Making Portion Of Our Program (Almost). What Awaits You Is A Lot Of Information, For Through Understanding Comes Enlightenment. Wow, That's Deep Stuff And I Can Sure Lay It On Deep!! You May Think That Is A Weird Way To Begin, But It Was Necessary. A Simple "D" Bow Is A Complex Bit Of Engineering And It Is My Goal To Shock You Into Thinking About The

38

MANY FACTORS THAT WILL LINE UP GIVING
YOU THE ABILITY TO CRAFT A GOOD
WORKING BOW.

NOW THAT YOU ARE BRACED FOR A
TRIP THROUGH A LABYRINTH OF TANGENTS,
YOUR FIRST LESSON IS THAT A BOW,
ANY BOW IS NOTHING MORE THAN A
SPRING... AN ENERGY STORAGE AND
RELEASE MECHANISM THAT IS BOUND
BY THE PHYSICAL LIMITATIONS OF THAT
WOOD IT IS MADE FROM, THE DESIGN
OF THE BOW : LENGTH, WIDTH, THICKNESS,
TAPER, MASS OF TIPS, CROSS SECTION, QUALITY
OF TILLERING (ITS BEND), MOISTURE LEVEL
OF THE WOOD, PHASE OF THE MOON,...
A LOT OF THINGS YOU MUST BEGIN
THINKING ABOUT. A QUESTION MOST
ASKED IS, "CAN THIS WOOD BE MADE
INTO A BOW?". WITHOUT KNOWING
WHAT THE WOOD IS, MY ANSWER IS,
"YES, BUT YOU NEED TO DESIGN THE BOW
AROUND THE WOOD."

THE "D" BOW IS THE SIMPLEST
FORM OF SPRING, I MEAN BOW. AGAIN,
IT IS SHAPED LIKE THE LETTER D
WHEN STRUNG, OR AS WE BOW PEOPLE
SAY, BRACED. A D BOW MAKES FULL

USE OF IT'S LENGTH BENDING FROM TIP
TO TIP, JUST LIKE A LEAF SPRING.
THE NIFTY THING ABOUT THESE BOWS
IS NOT JUST THEIR SIMPLICITY, BEING
LITTLE MORE THAN A WELL TAPERED
STRIP OF WOOD, THEY CAN BE SHORTER
THEN THEIR STIFF HANDLED BRETHREN
WHILE MAINTAINING THE SAME DRAW
LENGTH. THEY CAN DO THIS BECAUSE THEY
HAVE SIMILAR LENGTHS OF BENDING
WOOD.

THIS IS ALL PRETTY SIMPLE STUFF
TO ABSORB BUT REREAD IT AGAIN AND
AGAIN UNTIL IT SOAKS INTO YOUR DNA
BECAUSE THOSE SIMPLE THOUGHTS WILL
CARRY YOU INTO THE LAND OF TANGENTS.

CLOSE YOUR EYES AND VISUALIZE A
D BOW FROM THE SIDE, BEING DRAWN.
IF IT HELPS, PICTURE SOMEONE WHO
WILL DRAW YOUR INTEREST PULLING IT
BACK THEN ALLOWING IT TO GO BACK
SLOWLY TO IT'S BRACED POSITION. RINSE
AND REPEAT.

PARDEN MY HARSHNESS BUT IF YOU
ARE SAYING THAT YOUR MIND DOESN'T WORK
THAT WAY.... YOU CAN'T USE YOUR INNER

40

SIGHT LIKE A MOVIE THAT YOU DIRECT, MY
ANSWER WILL BE THE SAME AS IT IS
WHEN PEOPLE TELL ME THEY CAN'T
HANDLE A BOW STRING THAT IS TIED
ON — GET OVER YOURSELF AND PRACTICE
UNTIL YOU CAN. IT IS A NECESSARY
SKILL.

AS THAT BOW IS DRAWN INTO A
WELL TILLERED CURVE, SEE IN YOUR MIND'S
EYE HOW THE OUTSIDE, OR BACK OF THE
BOW IS STRETCHING: THE FIBERS ON THE
BACK ARE STORING ENERGY IN TENSION.
HICKORY BEING STRONGER IN TENSION THAN
CHERRY CAN STORE MORE ENERGY BEFORE
FAILURE. * MAKE A CHERRY BOW WIDER
TO MAKE IT HEAVIER. THE INSIDE OF
THE BOW, THE BELLY WHEN DRAWN IS
BEING COMPRESSED AND IS STORING ENERGY
AS A COIL SPRING WOULD DO AS YOU SQUISH
IT BETWEEN YOUR FINGERS. BLACK
LOCUST, THE CRUSHING STRENGTH CHAMP
CAN SURVIVE COMPRESSION FAILURE ON
A MUCH GRANDER SCALE THAN WHITE
ASH ... MAKE LOCUST BOWS NARROWER
THAN ASH BOWS.

THERE IN LIES A LESSON. WHETHER
YOU TRIED TO MAKE YOUR FIRST BOW, OR

41

YOU WERE TRYING TO MAKE A ROUND
BELLIED ENGLISH LONGBOW AND IT
FAILED IN EITHER COMPRESSION OR
TENSION, IT WASN'T RANDOM FATE
THAT DID IT IN, IT WAS EXACTLY
BECAUSE YOU DID NOT DESIGN YOUR
BOW WITHIN THE PHYSICAL LIMITATIONS
OF YOUR BOW WOOD,

(THE FOLLOWING IS INTENDED FOR A
SPECIFIC AUDIENCE : IF YOU ARE
STRUGGLING WITH MAKING ROUND
BELLIED WAR BOWS OUT OF WOODS
OTHER THAN YEW, AND THEY EITHER
KEEP BREAKING OR AT THE LEAST
SUFFERING MAJOR STRING FOLLOW, TRY
SOMETHING DIFFERENT. IT'S NO MORE
A SECRET NOW THAN IT WAS 500
YEARS AGO THAT WHITE ASH BOWS NEED
TO BE WIDER AND FLATTER THAN YEW
LONGBOWS... WHERE IS IT STATED THAT
ALL BOWS MUST HAVE A "D" SHAPED
CROSS SECTION? PROBABLY IN THE SAME
PLACE THAT SAYS WE SHOULD BURN
WITCHES AT THE STAKE AND STUMP WATER
CURES WARTS.)

        BY NOW YOU SHOULD HAVE PICKED UP
ON WHY MEMBERS OF THE TRADITIONAL BOW

CLAN LAMINATE HICKORY STRIPS TO THE BELLIES OF OTHER WOODS IN ORDER TO CREATE SUPER WOODS. WE MEMBERS OF THE PRIMITIVE BOW CLAN SHUN GLUING WOOD TOGETHER (RISERS ON BOARD BOWS ARE FORGIVEN), SO WE BACK BOWS WITH RAWHIDE OR SINEW: THAT MAGICAL MATERIAL BLESSED WITH THE ABILITY TO STORE GREAT GOBS, YES I SAID GOBS, OF ENERGY IN TENSION. TENDONS ARE STRONG AND SINEW IS TENDONS.

BACK FROM THE BRINK OF THE TANGENT ABYSS: LYING BETWEEN THAT OUTER LAYER OF TENSION AND THAT INNER LAYER BEING COMPRESSED IS THE LAYER THAT DOES NEITHER. THIS IS THE NEUTRAL PLANE.

SO TO RECAP, WE NOW UNDERSTAND MANY THINGS: 1) A BOW IS A SPRING 2) A D BOW LOOKS LIKE A D, 3) THE BACK IS UNDER TENSION, THE BELLY IS UNDER COMPRESSION, AND THE NEUTRAL PLANE WATCHES NETFLIX. 4) DIFFERENT WOODS HAVE DIFFERENT CAPABILITIES, 5) IF YOU KEEP TRYING TO DO THE SAME THING OVER AND OVER EXPECTING DIFFERENT RESULTS..... GO WIDER AND FLATTER. YES I AM TALKING TO YOU.

YOUR NEXT ASSIGNMENT IS TO TAKE WHAT
YOU HAVE LEARNED SO FAR AND DELVE
DEEPER INTO BOW (SPRING) THEORY: LET US
TAKE A WOOD SUCH AS BLACK LOCUST, ONE
OF THE MMA FIGHTERS OF THE BOW WOOD
WORLD, THEN CHOOSE A LESS BEASTLY WOOD
SUCH AS BLACK WALNUT, AND SET A GOAL
OF BUILDING A 64" D BOW FROM EACH
WHICH DRAWS 50 POUNDS AT 27" (AIM FOR
DRAW LENGTHS LESS THAN HALF THEIR NOCK
TO NOCK LENGTHS, PLUS AN ADDED MARGIN
OF SAFETY).

SO FAR WE KNOW THAT BLACK LOCUST
IS STIFFER THAN WALNUT, SO LESS WOOD
IN BLACK LOCUST WILL STORE THE
SAME ENERGY AS MORE WOOD IN WALNUT.
WE ALSO KNOW THAT THE BEND RADIUS
OF EACH BOW WILL BE SIMILAR SIMPLY
BECAUSE OF GEOMETRY: SAME BOW LENGTH,
SAME DRAW, SAME BRACE HEIGHTS
(5½ INCHES, LOW BRACE IS YOUR FRIEND), ETC.
WE ALSO UNDERSTAND TENSION AND COMPRESSION.

IF WE HAVE A SIMILAR BEND RADIUS
(THE SAME AMOUNT AND DEGREE OF CURVE),
A SPECIFIC AMOUNT OF BENDING ON A 64"
BOW DRAWN TO 27" WILL DEVELOP. BECAUSE
OF THIS, THE ACTUAL AMOUNT OF STRETCHING

44

AND COMPRESSING COULD BE CALCULATED ON
THE OUTER SURFACES (GIVEN THE THICKNESS
AT EACH POINT ALONG THE LIMBS.
IT IS A DEFINITE AND MEASURABLE
AMOUNT OF STRETCH AND SQUISH WHICH
INCREASES ON THE BACK AND BELLY
SURFACES AS THE BOW IS MADE THICKER
AND LESSENS AS THE BOW IS MADE
THINNER (VERY IMPORTANT TO KNOW WHEN
DESIGNING BOWS! CONTROL THE AMOUNT
OF STRESS IN A WOODEN SPRING BY
STAYING WITHIN THE LIMITS OF THE WOOD
THROUGH THICKNESS).

 I SHALL REPEAT THIS AS IT IS
SO IMPORTANT; FOR A GIVEN MATERIAL,
THERE IS A LIMIT IN THICKNESS
THAT YOU CAN NOT EXCEED SO YOUR
OPTION IS TOO INCREASE WIDTH TO INCREASE
DRAW WEIGHT WHEN YOU ARE NEAR THE
WOOD'S LIMIT. ANOTHER OPTION IS TO INCREASE
THE LENGTH OF THE BOW, REDUCING BEND
RADIUS, ALLOWING THE WOOD TO BE THICKER. THIS
IS ALSO POSSIBLY A ROAD TO SLOWER CAST
(ARROW SPEED). AH HAA!! SO HOW DO YOU
MAKE VERY SHORT BOWS? MAKE THEM
WIDER AND THINNER.

 FOR OUR PURPOSES WE WILL STAY AS
SIMPLE AS POSSIBLE AND SAY THAT DIFFERENT

WOODS CAN ALL TAKE ABOUT THE SAME AMOUNT
OF STRETCH AND SQUISHING BEFORE FAILURE
HAPPENS. THAT IS NOT COMPLETELY TRUE AND
THERE ARE DEFINITE EXCEPTIONS (YEW),
BUT IT IS TRUE ENOUGH FOR THIS
DISCUSSION ON WHITE WOODS. IT IS MEANT
AS A STARTING POINT, AND AS YOU PROGRESS
THESE "TRAINING WHEELS" CAN BE TOSSED
ASIDE.

WHERE WERE WE? SHINY OBJECT....
LOOK AT THE SHINY OBJECT.....

THE MAGIC NUMBER SHALL BE A
LITTLE LESS THAN $\frac{1}{2}$". $\frac{1}{2}$" IS YOUR
MAGIC NUMBER FOR A BOW PLUS OR MINUS
64" IN LENGTH, FOR THE AVERAGE
THICKNESS OF THE LIMBS. FOR A PYRAMID
BOW, THE THICKNESS WILL BE CONSTANT
BECAUSE THE LIMB TILLERING IS CAUSED
BY AN EVEN TAPER IN WIDTH. FOR A
MORE PARALLEL LIMBED BOW, THE THICKNESS
IS GREATEST NEAR THE HANDLE AND
THINS TOWARDS THE TIPS, BUT IT WILL
BE AROUND $\frac{1}{2}$" MIDLIMB. THIS THICKNESS
IS CLOSE TO THE MAXIMUM FOR A 64"
BOW DRAWN TO 27", KEEPING TENSIONAL
AND COMPRESSIONAL MOVEMENT WITHIN LIMITS.

So RIDDLE ME THIS: IF YOU ARE LOOKING AT A LOCUST BOW AND A WALNUT BOW OF SIMILAR LENGTH AND DRAW WEIGHT, BOTH BEING THE MAGICAL ½ INCH IN THICKNESS HOW WOULD THEY DIFFER? YEP, IN WIDTH. THE LOCUST BOW WOULD BE A BIT NARROWER.

OF COURSE, DIFFERENT WOODS CAN TAKE DIFFERENT AMOUNTS OF TENSON AND COMPRESSION, YEW COMES TO MIND BECAUSE IT CAN HANDLE THICK AND ROUND CROSS SECTIONS WITH GRACE, BUT THE BASIC IDEAS I HAVE LAYED AT YOUR FEET TO PONDER FORM A GOOD WORKING THEORY. THEY ARE ALSO TRUE ENOUGH AT THEIR CORE TO FORM THE FOUNDATION OF YOUR KNOWLEDGE. THE BASIC SEEDS SHOULD BE PLANTED: BOWS MADE OF WEAKER WOODS NEED TO BE MADE WIDER THAN BOWS MADE OF STRONGER WOODS BECAUSE ADDING THICKNESS WITHOUT ADDING LENGTH WILL OVERSTRESS THE SPRING.

"WUD IS WUD"

BEFORE WE BEGIN, LET ME ASSURE YOU THAT THIS BOW COULD JUST AS EASILY BE MADE FROM A ¾" x 2" RED OAK BOARD, AS IT WOULD BE FROM A TREE YOU CUT IN YOUR BACK YARD. WOOD IS WOOD AND

AS LONG AS IT WASN'T RUINED THROUGH BAD
KILN PROCEDURES OR CUT FROM A SICK TREE
IT WILL BE FINE. THERE WAS A TIME
WHEN PEOPLE THOUGHT KILN DRYING KILLED
THE LIFE OF WOOD, THAT HAS BEEN
PROVEN TO BE FALSE. ALL YOU NEED TO
KNOW IS STRAIGHT LINES ARE YOUR
FRIEND. FOR MORE INFORMATION ON PICKING
A BOARD, SKIP AHEAD TO THE SECOND
PROJECT BOW WHERE I GO INTO GREATER
DETAIL.

"FINDING YOUR TREE"

* TANGENT ALERT *

    AIKIDO AS I UNDERSTAND, USES
ONE'S OPPONENT'S ENERGY AGAINST THEM.
THIS PHILOSOPHY IS DIFFERENT THAN A
SIMPLE "KEEP MOVING FOWARD AND THUMP"
THAT RELIES UPON RAW STRENGTH,.... THUMPING
POWER, AND TOUGHNESS,... ABILITY TO
SURVIVE A THUMPING. YEW IS THE AIKIDO
MASTER, WHILE OSAGE AND BLACK LOCUST
ARE THE LORDS OF THUMPING. ALL OTHERS
FALL SOMEWHERE ALONG THE THUMPING
SPECTRUM... JUNIPER BEING A COMBINATION.

    HOW THIS RELATES TO ANYTHING IS FOR
US TO FIGURE OUT, BUT I SHALL RELATE IT

TO CROSS SECTION: HOW DESIGN MEETS
MATERIAL MEETS THE SIZE OF THE STAVE.

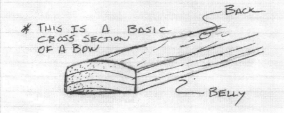

* THIS IS A BASIC
CROSS SECTION
OF A BOW

BACK

BELLY

IF WE ARE TO FOLLOW OUR CREED
"MAXIMIZE THE STRESS, BUT DON'T EXCEED
LIMITS", WE NEED TO UNDERSTAND HOW
THE WOOD IS MOVING THROUGHOUT A
CROSS SECTION. BY NOW WE ALL KNOW
THAT THE BACK IS UNDER TENSION
AND THE BELLY IS UNDER COMPRESSION.
INTUITIVELY WE SHOULD KNOW THAT BECAUSE
THERE IS AN AREA WHICH ISN'T UNDER
EITHER FORCE, THE NEUTRAL PLANE, THE
GREATEST FORCES ARE ON THE SURFACE WITH
FORCES DECREASING AS THEY MOVE TOWARD
THE NEUTRAL PLANE. THE THICKER THE
BOW, GIVEN A SPECIFIC BEND RADIUS (GEOMETRY),
THE GREATER THE FORCES ARE ALONG EACH
SURFACE. FORCES THAT HAVE DEFINITE
LIMITS... EACH WOOD HAS DEFINITE LIMITS.

49

GIVEN THAT A MATERIAL HAS A DEFINITE
AMOUNT OF TENSIONAL AND COMPRESSIONAL
MOVEMENT THAT IT CAN WITHSTAND
BEFORE IT SUFFERS DAMAGE OR
OUTRIGHT FAILS, WE CAN COMPARE
VARIOUS CROSS SECTIONS TO GET AN IDEA
OF HOW WELL THEY MAY SERVE US AS
BOW MAKERS.

THE FOLLOWING GRAPH COMPARES CROSS
SECTIONS WHICH ARE SOMEWHAT COMMON.
THE HORIZONTAL LINE REPRESENTS THE
NEUTRAL PLANE AND THE VERTICAL AXIS
REPRESENTS THE MAXIMUM THICKNESS OF
THE BOW (MAXIMUM AMOUNT OF LATERAL
MOVEMENT IN TENSION AND COMPRESSION)
FOR WHITE ASH. I COULD HAVE SAID
MULBERRY, OR OAK.... BUT LET'S GIVE A
REAL NAME TO THE WOOD, THE POINT
IS, FOR A GIVEN BEND RADIUS THERE
IS A MAXIMUM FOR THICKNESS REGARDLESS
OF THE PARTICULAR CROSS SECTION.
* THE NEUTRAL PLANE WILL SHIFT DEPENDING
ON THE CROSS SECTION, HOWEVER THE
RULES STILL APPLY.

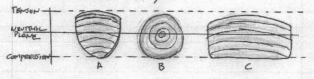

TENSION

NEUTRAL
PLANE

COMPRESSION

A   B   C

CROSS SECTION A) THIS IS THE CROSS SECTION OF
A PROPER ENGLISH LONGBOW AND HAS BEEN
USED OVER A LONG PERIOD OF TIME BECAUSE
IT IS EASY TO MAKE ALONG WITH HAVING
THE VALUE OF ECONOMY OF MATERIALS.
BEING NARROW IT CAN BE MADE FROM
SMALL DIAMETER STAVES, MAXIMIZE THE
NUMBER OF BOWS WHICH CAN BE MADE
FROM A LOG, AS WELL AS BEING QUICK
TO WORK INTO A BOW. A BIT OF TRIVIA
IS THAT A SMALL STAVE COULD BE
SPLIT WITH THE FLAT SIDE USED AS THE
BACK! BACKWARDS BOW!!

IT IS EASY TO SEE THAT THERE ISN'T MUCH
WOOD TO STORE ENERGY WHERE THE COMPRESSIONAL
FORCES ARE PEAKING: AT THAT EXACT POINT
WHERE FORCES ARE THE GREATEST, WE
ARE INTENTIONALLY CONCENTRATING THEM
ALONG A NARROW RIDGE. WITH A WOOD SUCH
AS WHITE ASH OR HAZEL (SIMILAR TO BIRCH),
IT IS NOT AN OPTIMAL CROSS SECTION FOR
UPPER WEIGHT BOWS. AN ALTERNATIVE IS
TO INCREASE LENGTH, REDUCING BEND
RADIUS WHICH IN TURN REDUCES POTENTIAL
CAST. LONGER LIMBS WILL BE SLOWER
LIMBS AFTER A POINT.

YEW THOUGH, WORKS WELL WITH THIS CROSS
SECTION. BEING THE AIKIDO OF BOW WOODS,

51

THE OUTER SURFACES ARE ABLE TO COMPRESS LIKE COIL SPRINGS ALLOWING THE DEEPER WOOD TO SHARE THE LOAD. WHITE ASH ALONG WITH OTHER WHITE WOODS CRUMPLE AT THE SURFACE CAUSING DAMAGE TO THE BOW. WIDER AND FLATTER MY FRIENDS, BOWS THAT ARE FLAT ARE NOT AN AMERICAN INVENTION.

CROSS SECTION B) SAY NO TO DRUGS AND THIS TYPE OF BOW. I REALLY CAN'T SAY ANYTHING POSITIVE ABOUT IT EXCEPT YOU CAN MAKE A BOW FROM A RAW TREE BRANCH WITHOUT A KNIFE.

CROSS SECTION C) FOR ANY WOOD BESIDES YEW, THIS IS THE BEST CROSS SECTION FOR DISTRIBUTING FORCES. FLAT BELLY TO SPREAD THE LOAD, IT REDUCES THE LENGTH TO EFFICIENT DIMENSIONS, AND ALLOWS BOWS TO BE HEAVY. I BELIEVE THE SLIGHT CROWN ACTUALLY HELPS TO SOME DEGREE BECAUSE IT'S ON THE TENSION SIDE, AND IF IT IS TOO HIGH, IN IN CASE OF A SMALL STAVE BOW — SCRAPE IT FLAT... DECROWN THE STAVE.

"Back to Finding Your Tree"

Consider this: the athletic peak of a bow wood can match that of a human.... 15 to 35 years of age. That may or may not be true, and even less true for a wood that needs to have a well developed amount of heartwood .... or yew... it had to be yewwww.... But it is a nice thought.

Where this nice thought helps us is in not choosing staves from very young trees — very young trees are growing quickly and being small, they haven't faced many years of life's stress. I need to drive this point home so I will keep trying: all the wood from a single species is not equal! Bow wood taken from the upper surface of a branch is more dense and much finer in rings than the lower section, and wood from both sides is more dense and finer grained than trunkwood. Trunk wood from a leaning tree is more dense and finer ringed than a straight, vertical tree, and a 15 year old tree is generally tougher than a 5 year old tree....

So if you have a choice between cutting a tree of absolute minimum size and one that is a bit older, take the older one... It not only has been bouncing around in the wind longer, the growth has begun to slow after those first years of youthful exuberance, giving you a tighter structure.

"The Search"

During today's search, I did a walk about, seeking out a tree that had a straight and clean trunk, 4 to 6 inches in diameter at the base. A tree of this size will yield multiple staves within multiple sections (more then one log to split). My goal was to score in this order of importance, either a striped maple, sugar maple, red oak, or birch. Birch is always my last choice because I don't like taking young, healthy birch trees. Luckily I found a nice red oak that was growing in an area of frequent high winds. When I harvested the tree and cut it into a clean five foot

SECTION AND A CLEAN SIX FOOT SECTION,
THE EFFECT FROM EXPOSURE TO WIND
WAS APPARENT: THE WINDWARD SIDE
HAD VERY TIGHT GROWTH RINGS AND I
CAN ASSUME VERY DENSE WOOD. THE
TIGHT SIDE WILL BE MADE INTO SINEW
BACKED BOWS, THE OTHER, SELF BOWS.

"SPLITTING STAVES"

IF ONE WAS TO WAIT FOR A RAW
SECTION OF TREE TO DRY: A ROUND, A
LOG, OR WHATEVER YOU WISH TO CALL IT,
IT WOULD TAKE A LONG TIME TO REACH
A MOISTURE LEVEL OF 9%. PERHAPS A
YEAR OR MORE. I APPRECIATE HOW GENERAL
THAT SOUNDS, AND WHEN ASKED TO
DESCRIBE IN HARD NUMBERS HOW LONG
IT TAKES TO FULLY DRY OR CURE A LOG,
STAVE, OR ROUGHED OUT BOW THAT'S
REALLY ALL THAT I AM ABLE TO DO.
HOW LONG IT WILL TAKE TO REACH THE
GOAL OF A 9% MOISTURE LEVEL DEPENDS
UPON ENVIRONMENTAL CONDITIONS, THE
SIZE OF THE PIECE, AND TO A DEGREE
THE SPECIES (RING POROUS, ETC.).
WHAT IS CERTAIN IS THAT LOGS TAKE
A VERY LONG TIME COMPARED TO SPLIT
STAVES, WHICH TAKE LONGER THAN ROUGHED

55

OUT BOWS, WHICH TAKE LONGER THAN MORE
FINISHED BOWS. WIND AND EXPOSURE TO
SUN LIGHT SPEEDS THE PROCESS, AND CAR
"KILN" DRYING SPEEDS IT UP EVEN
FASTER: IT COULD REDUCE CURING TIME
TO SEVERAL WEEKS. IT ALSO CAN OVER
DRY THE WOOD,.... NOTHING IS FREE.

MY ADVICE GOES TWO WAYS: CUT
AND SPLIT STAVES, REMOVE THE BARK
AND PAINT THE ENDS, AND FORGET
ABOUT THEM. IN AN ATTIC THAT IS
WARM AND DRY, IN A DRY CORNER
OF YOUR WORKSHOP, WHEREVER THEY
WILL BE DRY AND PROTECTED. IF
THEY STAY FOR A YEAR, OR TEN YEARS
BEFORE YOU FIND THEM, CONSIDER THEM
AN EARLY BIRTHDAY PRESENT. IF YOU
WISH TO MAKE A BOW AND NOT
WAIT SO LONG, SPLIT YOUR STAVES AND
WORK THEM INTO ROUGHED OUT BOWS.
WORK ONE OF THEM DOWN, LET THE
BOW DRY IN THE DARK FOR A DAY OR
TWO, EXPOSED IT TO THE WEATHER FOR
A FEW WEEKS, AND THEN BABY IT
FOR A MONTH OR SO TO LET IT FULLY
CURE. ASIDE FROM THAT, THE ONLY SURE
WAY IS USING A MOISTURE METER: EITHER
GIVE IT YOUR BEST GUESS, OR ACTULLY MEASURE
IT.

IF THE FOLLOWING IS NEW TO YOU AND
YOU FIND IT TO BE USEFUL, THEN IT,
AND IT ALONE WILL MAKE READING
THROUGH MY RAMBLINGS WORTH THE PRICE
OF ADMISSION : GREEN BOWS ARE MALEABLE,
GREEN BOWS ARE OPEN TO SUGGESTION.
ONE CAN QUICKLY WORK A PIECE OF A
TREE INTO A RAW BOW SHAPE AND
THEN LASH IT TO A BOARD IN ANY WAY
YOU WISH TO SHAPE IT:

YOU COULD LASH IT TO THE BOARD
TO CENTER THE HANDLE BETWEEN THE
TIPS, LASH IT INTO REFLEX, LASH IT
TO FORM RECURVES, INTO A GULL WING
SHAPE, REFLEX DEFLEX, OR WHATEVER
YOU CAN COME UP WITH. JUST MAKE SURE
TO WORK THE BENDS IN SLOWLY, BOILING
OR STEAMING FOR SEVERE BENDS, AND
"OVER BEND" IT BECAUSE THERE WILL
BE SOME REBOUND. THIS, MY FRIENDS IS
A VALUABLE TECHNIQUE.

SPLITTING? ACTUAL SPLITTING AS I
SUGGESTING BEFORE GOING OFF ON TANGENTS?
OUT OF EVERYTHING DISCUSSED SO FAR,
SPLITTING IS SIMPLE. USE WEDGES, A
KNIFE, START AT THE END, IN THE
MIDDLE, START THE SPLIT WITH A

57

CHAINSAW.... WOODS WORK DIFFERENTLY SO
THERE IS NO ONE BEST WAY. SOMETIMES
THERE ARE LOTS OF GOOD WAYS, SINCE
LET'S FACE IT, IT'S NOT ROCKET
SURGERY OR BRAIN SCIENCE. THIS IS
YOUR BALL OF TWINE TO UNROLL. JUST
MAKE SURE THAT YOU STUDY YOUR LOG
FROM EVERY ANGLE AND USE A STRING
TO FIND OUT HOW TO GET THAT HANDLE
CENTERED BETWEEN THE TIPS.

I AM A MISER. I ATTEMPT TO GET
AS MANY BOWS FROM A LOG AS I
POSSIBLY CAN. THE GREATEST RISK OF
THIS IS LOSING THE ENTIRE LOG. IF
YOU ARE JUST STARTING OUT, DON'T BE
GREEDY. WITH EXPERIENCE COMES A
GREATER ABILITY TO GAIN EFFICIENCY.
IF YOU HAVE A CHOICE OF MAKING ONE
BOW SAFELY, OR SQEAKING THREE BOWS
FROM A STAVE POSSIBLY, GO FOR ONE
BOW.

"ROUGHING OUT THE BOW"

IT WOULD HELP TO KNOW TWO THINGS:
THAT CREATING THE SHAPE OF THE FACE
WILL BE REFFERED TO AS "WORKING THE
FACE", AND WORKING TO THE TARGET
THICKNESS SHALL BE REFERRED TO AS

"WORKING THE THICKNESS". SIMPLE, EH?

WITH ANY BOW I MAKE I WORK IN STAGES, EACH SECESSIVE REPEATING OF A STAGE SPEEDS UP AS I CLOSE IN ON THE FINISHED BOW. BY THIS I MEAN ROUGHING OUT THE FACE, THEN ROUGHING OUT THE THICKNESS.... THIS IS THE SLOW WORK BECAUSE A LOT OF WOOD NEEDS TO BE REMOVED. THEN I GO BACK TO WORKING THE FACE TO MY LINES WHICH GOES FASTER BECAUSE IT'S THINNER, THEN FINE TUNE THE THICKNESS....

"TIME TO BUILD A "D" BOW"

I STILL HAVE THE VERY FIRST BOW THAT I EVER MADE THAT WORKED WITHOUT BREAKING. IT WAS A GOOD TEACHER THOUGH IT WAS VERY LIGHT. IF THIS IS YOUR FIRST BOW, DON'T BASE YOUR SUCCESS OR FAILURE ON NAILING A SPECIFIC DRAW WEIGHT, BASE IT ON MAKING A WORKING BOW WITH A GOOD UNIFORM BEND. BASE IT ON LEARNING SOMETHING EVERY TIME YOU BUILD A BOW. I AM NOT ABLE TO GIVE YOU EXACT DIMENSIONS FOR A BOW INTENDED FOR A SPECIFIC DRAW LENGTH BECAUSE WOOD VARIES SO MUCH. WHAT

I CAN DO IS GIVE YOU SAFE DIMENSIONS
WHICH WILL WORK WITH A VARIETY OF
WOODS. FOLLOWING MY NUMBERS WILL
ALLOW YOU TO PUT TOGETHER A BOW
WITHIN A RANGE OF 35 TO 50 POUNDS
AT UP TO 27 INCHES OF DRAW. THIS
BY ANY STANDARDS CONSTITUTES A
WORKING BOW.

STEP 1) DRAWING YOUR LINES:

HISTORICALLY, THE NATIVES OF NORTH AMERICA
MADE D BOWS RANGING FROM VERY SHORT
TO VERY LONG, IN THE CASE OF CHEROKEE
WAR BOWS. *TANGENT: ENGLISH WARBOWS,
CHEROKEE WAR BOWS, AND BASSA WARBOWS
WERE DESIGNED FOR ARTILLERY SHOOTING
AND EVOLVED INTO SIMILAR FORMS....
THAT'S JUST AN INTERESTING OBSERVATION.

IN OUR CASE, I AM CHOOSING TO
MAKE OUR PROJECT BOW 64 INCHES LONG
SO WE CAN USE A FULL, ANCHORED
DRAW AND $1\frac{3}{8}$ INCHES WIDE AT THE
CENTER OF THE HANDLE TO ALLOW
ENOUGH WIDTH TO ACHIEVE HUNTING
WORTHY DRAW WEIGHTS WITH A WIDE
RANGE OF WOODS, YET STILL ALLOW THE
ARROW TO BEND AROUND THE HANDLE.

WHETHER YOUR STAVE BEGINS LIKE THIS:

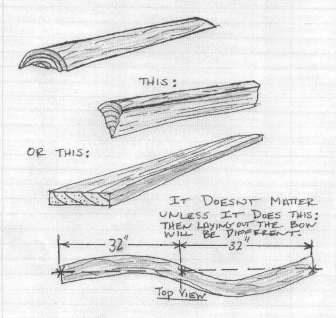

THIS:

OR THIS:

IT DOESN'T MATTER
UNLESS IT DOES THIS:
THEN LAYING OUT THE BOW
WILL BE DIFFERENT.

Top View

AS ODD AS IT MAY SEEM, ALL THAT
MATTERS (WITHIN REASON) IS THAT THE
CENTER OF THE HANDLE LINES UP WITH
THE CENTER OF THE TIPS. WHAT THE
LIMBS DO BETWEEN THOSE POINTS DOES
NOT REALLY MATTER.

62

I WILL GET TO HOW I HANDLE SNAKEY
STAVES IN A BIT, BUT FOR NOT WE WILL
LAY OUR BOWS OUT ON A STRAIGHT STAVE
(OR BOARD).

OUR DIMENSIONS WILL BE: 64" TIP TO TIP,
$1\frac{3}{8}$" CENTER HANDLE, TAPERING TO $\frac{7}{8}$"
AT EACH TIP. IF YOU ARE WONDERING,
THESE NUMBERS ARE NOT SUPER CRITICAL
UNLESS YOU ARE AIMING FOR MAKING A
BOW THAT MAXIMIZES IT'S PERFORMANCE
AT A SPECIFIC DRAW WEIGHT, FROM
A SPECIFIC WOOD.

*IF THE STAVE IS SNAKEY, YOU MAY
HAVE TO FIGURE IN THE CENTERING OF
THE HANDLE THROUGH THE TIPS BEFORE
CUTTING TO LENGTH. YOU MAY EVEN HAVE
TO REDUCE IT BEYOND 64" OR CUT IT
LONGER TO FIND A WAY TO CENTER
THINGS. YOU MAY HAVE TO MAKE ONE LIMB
LONGER THAN OTHER.... BUT IF YOUR STAVE
IS STRAIGHT, FIND THE CENTER LINE OF
YOUR STAVE AND USING A STRING AND
A SHARPY, MARK CENTER OF HANDLE AND
TIPS.

2) AFTER THE CENTER OF THE HANDLE
AND CENTERS OF TIPS ARE MARKED, AS
PRECISELY AS YOU POSSIBLY CAN, MAKE
WIDTH MARKS, FOLLOWED BY DRAWING THE
FACE SHAPE USING A STRAIGHT EDGE.

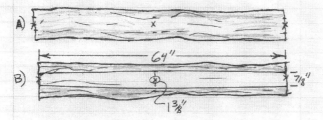

3) HOW YOU REDUCE THE STAVE AT THIS
POINT IS YOUR CHOICE: HATCHET, BANDSAW,
FERRIERS RASP, THEY ALL REMOVE WOOD.
IF THE STAVE IS SNAKEY, A DRAWKNIFE
IS A GOOD TOOL TO USE BECAUSE IT ALLOWS
YOU TO FOLLOW FIBERS. AS A BEGINNER,
ROUGHING OUT THE STAVE WITH A HATCHET,
FOLLOWED BY RASPING, FOLLOWED BY SANDING
IS A GOOD WAY TO GO: YOU CAN WORK UP
TO THE LINE, (DO NOT TOUCH THE LINE YET)
AND GET A SMOOTH ENOUGH SURFACE TO
SCRIBE A ROUGH THICKNESS LINE.

* AT THIS POINT, GIVE YOURSELF A SAFETY
MARGIN: LEAVE SPACE BETWEEN THE
EDGE OF THE WOOD AND YOUR LINE.

64

* BEFORE WE GO TOO FAR I SHOULD
MENTION HOW I DEAL WITH A SNAKEY
STAVE

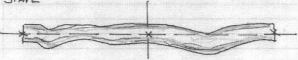

OPTION (1) AFTER USING A DRAWKNIFE ALONG
ONE EDGE OF THE STAVE TO LOCATE
THE TRUE LINE OF FIBERS, I USE A
STRING TO FIND A WAY TO ALIGN THE
BOW WITHIN THE STAVE, FOLLOWING THE
LENGTHWISE LINE OF FIBERS. AS ALWAYS,
IT IS OF GREAT IMPORTANCE TO MAKE
SURE HANDLE CENTER IS IN LINE
WITH BOW TIP CENTERS. IF YOU CAN DO
THIS WITHOUT CUTTING LENGTH FROM
YOUR STAVE CONSIDER YOURSELF LUCKY.

THE NEXT STEP I TAKE (IF IT'S A
CLEAN STAVE WITHOUT KNOTS) IS TO SCRIBE
A PARALLEL LINE WITH MY SCRIBING TOOL,
FOLLOWING THE DRAWKNIFED EDGE.
SCRIBE THIS LINE GIVING YOURSELF
ALLOWANCE TO ADJUST THE WIDTH AND
ALLIGNMENT. * WORKING KNOTTY STAVES
TAKES ADDED STEPS.

OPTION (2) IN OPTION (1), I CARRIED YOU
TO A CERTAIN POINT: WORKING THE
STAVE DOWN TO A ROUGHED OUT BOW
WIDTH. THE TIPS ARE NOT TAPERED
YET SO USE THE SAME FORM OF A
TEMPLATE AS YOU COULD USE FOR ANY
STAVE — STRAIGHT OR SNAKEY.

I AM A FAN OF TEMPLATES. A
TEMPLATE IS SIMPLY A SHAPE THAT
ONE USES TO MARK LINES ONTO THE
STAVE. I USE THEM FOR LIMB
SHAPES, HANDLE PROFILES, AND TIPS.
THEY CAN BE MADE FROM THIN
RIPPED BOARDS, 1/4" PLYWOOD, OR
POSTER BOARD. FOR SMALL SHAPES I
USE CARDBOARD FROM CEREAL BOXES.

ALTHOUGH TEMPLATES ARE STRAIGHT
AND TRUE, THEY CAN BE USED
ON SNAKEY PIECES BY STARTING
AT ONE END AND MARKING ALONG
IT'S EDGES IN SHORT SECTIONS.
ROTATE IT ALONG THE LENGTH OF
THE STAVE KEEPING IT CENTERED
ALONG THE WAY, ENDING UP WITH
THE TIP CENTER OF THE TEMPLATE
OVER THE TIP CENTER OF THE STAVE.

66

4) At every point in your project, ask yourself, "Have I goofed up". There are really a limited number of ways at this point that something could have gone off the tracks; the handle wont line up with the tips, you went within your lines, or when you were working to your lines you didn't angle the sides correctly which in effect means that you went within your lines..... Let me explain through the careful use of art...

Before doing a single thing beyond splitting your stave will look something like this

Or this

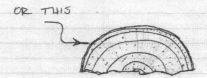

So far, we haven't goofed up?

    Yes ☐   No ☒ , Proceed to the next step guilt free.....

WITH THE MYSTERIOUS AND INVISIBLE LINES
ADDED TO OUR STAVE WE
CAN SEE WHERE THE STAVE
IS TO BE REDUCED TO FOR
A COMPLETED FACE PROFILE.

WHAT WE WANT AT THIS POINT
IS TO WORK DOWN TO THIS,
LEAVING A SMALL BIT OF EXTRA
WOOD AS A BUFFER.

LINE OF FINISHED WIDTH

SO FAR, WE HAVEN'T GOOFED UP?

☐ YES   ☒ NO , PROCEED TO THE
NEXT STEP.

IF WE DIDN'T WATCH
OUR ANGLES AND THIS
HAPPENED, WE GOOFED UP.
ANYWHERE ALONG THE
LENGTH, TO ANY DEGREE,
WE GOOFED UP AND WE
HAVE TO MAKE THE BOW
MORE NARROW.

WE GOOFED   ☒ YES ☐ NO

68

LUCKILY, YOU READ AHEAD TO AT LEAST THIS
POINT SO YOU UNDERSTAND THE VALUE OF
STAYING OUTSIDE OF THE LINES. IF YOU
HAVE TO ANGLE THE SIDES, ANGLE THEM
AWAY FROM YOUR LINES, THAT'S OK. IF
YOU DO GO INSIDE OF YOUR LINES, THE
ONLY THING YOU CAN DO IS NARROW THE
BOW. THAT MAY NOT BE A FATAL MISTAKE
BUT IF YOU DID..... NOT GOOD... STAY
OUTSIDE OF YOUR LINES!!

5) TIME TO THIN DA BOW!! I LOVE MY
SCRIBOMATIC. BEFORE I MADE VARIOUS TOOLS
FOR SCRIBING THICKNESS LINES, I WOULD
CUT STRIPS OUT OF CEREAL BOXES OF
THE DESIRED WIDTH AND CHASED THEM
DOWN THE SIDES OF THE BOWS. IT
WORKS. BUT, INVEST THE TIME TO BUILD
A TOOL FOR SCRIBING BECAUSE IT IS
OH SO HELPFUL.

$\frac{1}{2}$" IS MY MAGIC NUMBER. OF COURSE
WOODS VARY IN STIFFNESS BUT $\frac{1}{2}$" OR
BETTER YET, ABOUT $\frac{1}{2}$" IS A REALLY
GOOD STARTING POINT. NEVER FEAR, EVEN
THOUGH THE BOW WILL TAPER IN THICKNESS
FROM HANDLE TO TIP WE WILL KEEP
THAT IN MIND AS WE WORK.

WE SHALL REMEMBER, FOREVER BURNED
INTO OUR MINDS, THE FOLLOWING NUMBERS:
64, 16, 8, 1, 3/4, 1/2. NOW I'M GONNA
DRAW A BOX.....

SIDE VIEW

NOW I'M GONNA DRAW BOXES IN THAT
BOX....

8"

SIDE VIEW

16"   64"

IF YOU'RE ON THE BEAM, YOU'VE REALIZED
THAT WE ARE LOOKING AT THE SIDE
OF THE STAVE. THE CENTER/HANDLE
IS IN THE 8" ZONE. EVERYTHING IS
CENTERED. THE 1" WILL BE SCRIBED
WITHIN THE 8" BOX, 3/4" WITHIN THE
16" BOX, AND THE BULK OF THE LIMB
LENGTH SCRIBED TO 1/2".

BACK

BELLY

ABSORB THIS AND PREPARE TO DO "EYE WORK".

70

I ACTUALLY JUST SCRIBE ONE LINE AND
DO THE THICKENING OF THE HANDLE BY
EYE. THOUGH THESE BOXES FORM STEPS,
USE THE LINES AS REFERENCE LINES,
FORMING A TAPER: IN THE CENTER
OF THE BOW, IT IS A FULL INCH,
GRADING INTO THE 3/4", GRADING INTO
THE 1/2".

WITH YOUR THICKNESS LINES DRAWN, EITHER
WITH A SCRIBOMATIC, CARD BOARD STRIP,
OR COMPASS, IT'S TIME TO WORK THE BOW
TO A ROUGH THICKNESS. AGAIN, DO NOT
WORK DOWN TO LINES. WORK TO THE
POINT WHERE YOU SEE A SLIGHT BIT OF
WOOD ABOVE THE LINE. WHEN YOU GET
WITHIN 8" OF THE TIPS, FEEL FREE TO
TOUCH THE LINE.

WORK IN STAGES... BEVEL, BEVEL,
FLAT.

76

My favored way to bevel, bevel, flat
is by clamping the stave sidways
so I am looking straight down at
it while I use my Ferriers rasp.
After both sides are beveled I
clamp the piece so it is flat,
belly side up and using lighting
to see as best as possible, work
the belly flat, working from tip
to handle, rasp, scrape, sand.

Except for the tips and where the
steps are in the center section,
do not touch the lines.

6) If you are working a green stave
you may give it a very gentle bend
but no more than a very slight
bend. No is not the time to risk
damaging your work. It is time to
either take a break or better
yet, work another stave into a
bow.

Drying time will vary and the one
true way to guage moisture level
is with a moisture guage. However,
if you allow the bow to dry in
the wind and sunshine in a
moderately humid/dry place in

72

SEVERAL WEEKS IT WILL BE DRY
ENOUGH TO WORK. GIVE IT ANOTHER
MONTH TO DRY BEFORE YOU ACTUALLY
PUT A LOT OF PRESSURE ON IT,,,,
ALMOST FULL DRAW — 27" IS FULL
DRAW, AND NOT SHOOTING 300 ARROWS
A DAY. BABY IT FOR A WHILE.
I SPEED DRY BOWS IN MY CAR
PARKED IN FULL SUNLIGHT. I
BASICALLY BAKE THE HECK OUT OF
IT. IN THE WINTER, I BAKE SINEW
BACKED BOW ON A CEILING RACK
OVER A WOODSTOVE BUT IT ALSO
WORKS FOR STAVE DRYING. GIVEN
THE CHOICE I WOULD RATHER GO
WITH RELENTLESS BAKED BOWS OVER
USING THEM TOO GREEN. IF YOU ARE
IN AN ARID ENVIRONMENT YOUR
DANGER MAY ACTUALLY OVER DRYING,
BUT THIS CAN GET TOO HEAVY REALLY
FAST,,, ENOUGH SAID.

7) IT IS DEFINITELY TIME FOR PICTURES
TO BREAK UP ALL THIS CHATTER, BUT
THERE IS STILL MORE TO WRITE: TIME
TO WORK THE FACE EXACTY TO THE
LINES. I ACTUALLY SAND THE FACE AND
OR PEEL OFF ANY REMAINING INNER
BARK OVER A TEA KETTLE AND A
THUMB NAIL AT THIS POINT, AND

73

REDRAW MY FACE PROFILE WITH A VERY
SHARP PENCIL. IT MUST BE ACCURATE.
I STILL USE MY RASP, BUT I CAN
UNSCREW THE HANDLE ON MY FERRIERS
RASP MAKING IT EASY TO WORK WITH
LENGTHWISE. BEING ABLE TO HOLD IT
LENGTHWISE AGAINST THE SIDE OF THE
BOW MAKES WORKING A LONG EDGE
MORE PRECISE. I ALSO USE MY LONG
SANDING BLOCK FOR THIS PROCESS.

8) TIPS AND STRING GROOVES. UGLY TIPS
CAN WORK AS WELL AS NICE TIPS BUT LET'S
GO WITH NICE TIPS. A GOOD WAY TO
FIDDLE WITH DESIGNS IS SKETCHING OF
COURSE BUT TRY CUTTING BOW WIDTH
STRIPS OF CEREAL BOX CARDBOARD FOR
TEMPLATES AND MOCK UPS.

BELOW ARE A FEW OF MY FAVORITE
STYLES:

BEVEL

SCOOPED
OUT LIKE
A SPOON

BURNED IN
WITH A WIRE
HEATED WITH
A TORCH

74

IN THE INTEREST OF OVERCOMPLICATING THINGS
WE WILL GO ABOUT MAKING STRING GROOVES
AND REFINING THE TIPS. PARDEN MY
PENMANSHIP, I'M ON HOUR 14 OF WRITING
TODAY.

(A) I CLAMP THE BOW SECURELY BACK
SIDE UP AND MARK TWO TICK MARKS
EITHER 3/4" OR 1" FROM THE ENDS. IT
DEPENDS ON WHAT STYLE I AM DOING.

(B) USING MY 3/16" ROUND RASP I MAKE
AND ANGLED GROOVE ON EITHER SIDE AND
BEING VERY CAREFUL, MAKE ONE ON THE
OTHER SIDE DEAD EVEN WITH THE FIRST
ONE. DO NOT MAKE THEM DEEP. MAKING
EVERYTHING SHALLOW AT THIS POINT ALLOWS
SOME ADJUSTMENT.

(C) MAKE SHALLOW
GROOVES AT AN
ANGLE ON
EACH SIDE

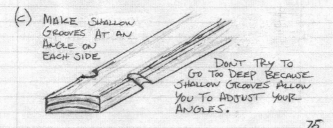

DON'T TRY TO
GO TOO DEEP BECAUSE
SHALLOW GROOVES ALLOW
YOU TO ADJUST YOUR
ANGLES.

75

(D) CLAMP THE BOW BELLY SIDE UP AND CAREFULLY DEEPEN THE GROOVES, ADJUSTING THEM (YOU CAN BECAUSE THEY WERE NOT VERY DEEP) SO THEY ARE EVEN, CARRYING THEM FARTHER INTO THE BELLY THAN YOU DID ON THE BACK.

(E) FINISH UP BY CLAMPING THE BOW, BACK SIDE UP, AND WITH A ROCKING MOTION, ROUND THE GROOVES AS THEY PASS FROM THE BACK TO THE BELLY. END THAT BY WRAPPING A PIECE OF 120 OR 220 GRIT AROUND THE SMALL END OF THE RASP AND SMOOTH THE GROOVES. SOFTEN THE SHARP EDGES OF THE GROOVES WITH SANDPAPER.

(F) AT THIS POINT I REFINE THE TIPS WITH A RASP FOLLOWED WITH A SANDING BLOCK.

(G) TAKE A BREAK AND WATCH ONE OF MY VIDEOS ON YOUTUBE.....

9) PRE - TILLERING TIME! THIS IS THE TIME BOW BEAUTIFICATION. I CAN SAY THIS WITH A STRAIGHT FACE BECAUSE THERE IS BEAUTY IN FUNCTION AS THERE IS IN A BOW WITH ROUNDED EDGES, A SMOOTH TAPER, AND THE LAY OF GROWTH RINGS ALONG THE BELLY (STAVE BOWS).

* BOARD BOW P.T. — BOARD BOW PRE-T'ING TO ME INCLUDES ROUNING OFF THE BACK. MY SENSE OF STYLE DOESN'T INCLUDE A DEAD FLAT BACK. THAT JUST LOOKS TO "BOARD LIKE". MY FIRST STEP IS TO BEVEL THE EDGES.....

* BEVELS IN DIAGRAM ARE EXAGGERATED FOR CLARITY

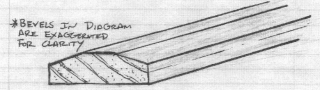

THE REASON WHY I BEVEL BEFORE ROUNDING IS BECAUSE CLEAN BEVEL LINES ARE GOOD REFERENCE LINES, THE KEY TO UNIFORM ROUNDING - THE NEXT STEP. I ALSO ROUND THE EDGES....

77

THE REASONS WHY I ROUND THE BACK ARE
BECAUSE IT RELIEVES STRESS ALONG THE
EDGES ALONG WITH MAKING THE BOW LOOK
MORE ORGANIC. IT DOESN'T TAKE MUCH
ROUNDING TO MAKE A VISUAL DIFFERENCE
SO GO EASY AT FIRST. SOME PEOPLE
JUST BEVEL AND THAT IS CALLED
"TRAPPING".... MAKING THE CROSS SECTION
TRAPEZOIDAL IN SHAPE.

* STAVE BOW P.T. — STAVE BOW PRE-
T'ING DOESN'T INCLUDE THE BEVELS
BUT IT DOES INCLUDE WORKING ON THE
BACK: ROUNDING THE EDGES AND FINISH
SANDING. I'LL MAKE SURE THE BACK IS
SILKY SMOOTH AT THIS POINT, INCLUDING
REFINING THE TIPS. IT'S NICE TO HAVE
ONE AREA FINISHED MORE OR LESS.

THE SIDES CAN ALSO BE WORKED UPON:
WITH GREAT CARE, MAKE SURE THAT UP
TO THIS POINT, YOUR THINNING IS
SYMETRICAL — BOTH LIMBS ARE WORKED THE
SAME. NOW IS THE TIME TO FINISH SAND
THE SIDES AND REMOVE ALL OF THE PENCIL
LINES AND USE GROWTH RINGS FOR
REFERENCE LINES ALONG WITH TRAINING
OUR EYES TO JUDGE TAPER.

78

(A) THE GROWTH RINGS SHOW UP ON THE
BELLY RESEMBLING A TOPOGRAPHIC MAP.
THEY WILL APPEAR AS "V's" POINTING
"DOWNHILL". UNLESS THE STAVE HAD VERY
ODD GROWTH, EVEN WIGGLEY AND
WONKEY STAVES WILL WORK THIS WAY.

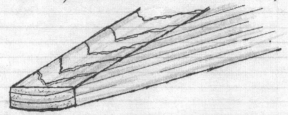

(B) ON A SIMPLE BOW LIKE THIS, THE LAY
AND INTERVALS OF THE "V's" ALONG WITH
JUDGING TAPER MAKES PRE-TILLERING AS
EASY AS IT COULD POSSIBLY BE. USING A
SANDING BLOCK AND YOUR EYES GETTING
ENOUGH TAPER BEFORE GIVING YOUR BOW
IT'S FIRST BEND IS PRETTY SIMPLE.
WITH A SANDING BLOCK......

SPACE THE "V's" AND KEEP THE POINTS
CENTERED. ✱ DON'T OVERWORK THE HANDLE!

79

I SUGGEST SAVING THE HANDLE AREA
FOR LATER. THIS IS A RISKIER AREA TO
WORK DURING PRE-TILLERING BECAUSE
HAVING TOO MUCH BEND THROUGH THE
HANDLE IS A BOW KILLER.

* IF YOU ARE JUST STARTING OUT, TEMPER
PRE-TILLERING. I CAN BASICALLY MAKE
A BOW WITHOUT EVER TOUCHING A
TILLERING STICK AND USE THE TILLERING
STICK JUST TO FINE TUNE THE LIMBS.
AS A BEGINNING BOW MAKER BE MORE
CONSERVATIVE : ROUGH OUT THE TAPER
AND GROWTH RING SPACING, SAVING THE
FINE TUNING FOR THE TILLERING STICK.

10) A BOW IS NOT MADE, IT IS TILLERED.
HOW DO WE AVOID THE CURSE OF STRING
FOLLOW? HOW DO WE KEEP THE BOW
FROM BREAKING? HOW DO WE MAXIMIZE
THE DRAW WEIGHT, EFFICIENCY, ARROW
CAST? HOW DO WE TURN THIS BOW INTO
THE BEST POSSIBLE BOW IT COULD BE?
PROPER TILLERING. THAT IS MY FINAL ANSWER.
PROPER TILLERING BOTH IN THE PROCESS
OF DEVELOPING THE BEND AND THE PROFILE
OF THE COMPLETED BEND. UP TILL NOW
WE HAVE BEEN PREPARING. NOW WE WILL
DO.

(A) CONCEPTS TO BARE IN MIND ARE
THAT YOU SHOULD ONLY BEND THE BOW
ENOUGH TO SEE HOW IT BENDS. I
HAVE HEARD FROM DIFFERENT SOURCES
TO BEND IT NO FARTHER THAN THE
TARGET DRAW WEIGHT. TO PULL IT BACK
8 INCHES. TO PULL IT BACK A % OF
IT'S TARGET DRAW LENGTH. I DON'T
AGREE. I PULL IT BACK ONLY FAR
ENOUGH TO SEE ENOUGH BEND THAT WILL
ALLOW ME TO JUDGE HOW TO REMOVE
MATERIAL. BABY YOUR BOW AND WORK
CAREFULLY.

ANOTHER THING TO BARE IN MIND IS
THAT SOMETIMES OUR MINDS CAN SCREAM
"STOP" BUT OUR HANDS DON'T LISTEN.
TRAIN YOUR HANDS TO STOP WHEN TOLD
TO AND TAKE A BREAK. OTHER TRICKS
INCLUDE FLEXING THE BOW GENTLY TEN
OR MORE TIMES EVERY TIME YOU REMOVE
MATERIAL SO THE BOW CAN FULLY RESPOND
TO CHANGE, AND TRAIN YOURSELF TO COUNT
SANDING STROKES.

YOU CAN CERTAINLY USE A RASP, SCRAPER,
OR SAND PAPER TO TILLER, BUT ON A
BOW LIKE THIS, WORKED TO THE LINES, I
PREFER 80 GRIT AND A SANDING BLOCK.

81

(B) WHEN I PLAN THE FINISHED SHAPE OF
THE BEND, DISTRIBUTING THE FORCES AS
EVENLY AS POSSIBLE IS MY GOAL. GO BACK
IN TIME TO OUR DISCUSSION ABOUT BEND
RADIUS AND THE ACTUAL MOVEMENT ALONG
THE SURFACES IN THE FORM OF TENSION
AND COMPRESSION. THEY ARE TIED TOGETHER.

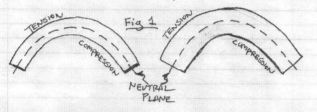

Fig 1

TENSION
COMPRESSION
TENSION
COMPRESSION
NEUTRAL PLANE

IN Fig 1, WONKEY SKETCHING ASIDE, THE TWO
SECTIONS OF BOW LIMBS HAVE THE SAME
BEND RADIUS. THEY DO NOT HAVE THE
SAME THICKNESS, THOUGH, SO THE WOOD
ON THE THICKER ONE IS FORCED TO STRETCH
AND COMPRESS TO A HIGHER DEGREE. IF
THE AMOUNT OF ACTUAL MOVEMENT OF THE
WOOD ALONG THE SURFACES OF THE THICKER
ONE ARE WITHIN THE LIMITS OF THE WOOD,
ALL IS GOOD EXCEPT THAT THE THINNER ONE
ISN'T WORKING AS HARD AS IT SHOULD.

IF THE THIN SECTION IS NEAR IT'S LIMIT,
YOU EITHER GET MAJOR STRING FOLLOW OR
A BROKEN BOW.

82

IN Fig2, LET'S ASSUME THAT MY SKETCH WAS
MADE ACCURATELY, HOWEVER THE CONCEPT
HOLDS TRUE:

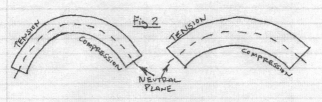

In THIS EXAMPLE, THE LIMB SECTION ON THE
LEFT IS THINNER THAN THE SECTION ON THE
RIGHT. BECAUSE THE THICKER SECTION HAS
LESS BEND, AND I DREW THEM BOTH PERFECTLY,
THE ACTUAL MOVEMENT ALONG ALL THE
SURFACES ARE SIMILAR IN TENSION AND
COMPRESSION. I DO REALIZE THAT I AM
OVER SIMPLIFYING THIS. IT IS A VERY
COMPLEX SYSTEM WITH MORE THAN A FEW
VARIABLES BUT I WANT TO GET YOU
THINKING ABOUT HOW THICKNESS RELATES
TO BEND.

(C) FORMS OF TILLER: I SHALL REFRAIN
FROM CALLING SOME TILLERS BAD AND SOME
TILLERS GOOD. SOME TILLERING IS ACTUALLY
BAD, BUT IT'S A SPECTRUM AND SOME
ARE WELL LIKED AND ARE COMMONLY USED.

83

IN THE INTEREST OF PLAYING WELL WITH OTHERS, I WILL SKIRT THE ISSUE OF PASSING JUDGEMENT USING THE WORD BAD.

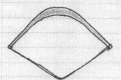

BENDING MOSTLY THROUGH THE HANDLE. I'M SORRY BUT THIS IS GENERALLY VERY BAD... BAD.

THERE ARE EXCEPTIONS AND THEY USUALLY CENTER AROUND VERY SHORT BOWS. THE BOW MAKERS WHO TILLER THESE TYPES OF BOWS, IF IT WORKS, HAVE THEIR REASONS, BUT IF THE BOWS ARE AVERAGE BOWS OF AVERAGE LENGTH TILLER SUCH AS THIS RESULTS IN HAND SHOCK AND BIG STRING FOLLOW.

WHIP TILLERING. BETTER THAN BENDING TOO MUCH THROUGH THE HANDLE BUT STILL NOT OPTIMUM. TOO MUCH OF THE BEND IS CONCENTRATED IN TOO SMALL AREAS.

*NOTE SOME SHORT BOWS HAVE DEFLEXED LIMBS WHICH RESEMBLE WHIP TILLERING.

84

<u>CIRCULAR OR COMPASS</u> TILLERING IS PRETTY. THE BEND IS SPREAD THROUGOUT THE LENGTH OF THE BOW, SO THIS FALLS INTO THE GREAT RANGE OF TILLERS. ENGLISH LONG BOWS AND WAR BOWS UTILIZE THIS BEND TO GOOD ADVANTAGE. IF YOUR D BOW FINISHES WITH THIS BEND... GREAT JOB!!

<u>ELLIPTICAL TILLER</u> IS MY FAVORITE FOR D BOWS. AS THE BOW BEGINS BENDING AT THE HANDLE, THE THICKEST PART, IT BARELY BENDS. AS IT THINS TOWARD THE TIPS, IT INCREASES IN BEND, KEEPING THE AMOUNTS OF TENSIONAL AND COMPRESSIONAL MOVEMENT MORE EVEN THROUGHOUT IT'S LENGTH.

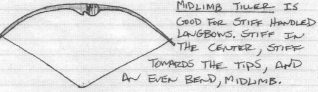

<u>MIDLIMB TILLER</u> IS GOOD FOR STIFF HANDLED LONGBOWS. STIFF IN THE CENTER, STIFF TOWARDS THE TIPS, AND AN EVEN BEND, MIDLIMB.

85

11) MAKING STRINGS, BOTH TILLERING AND
BOW. EVEN THOUGH I FAVOR SIMPLE TWO PLY
STRINGS THE HAVE ONE LOOP AND ONE END
THAT IS TIED TO THE BOW, WITH MY
SKETCHING ABILITY THIS NEXT PART WILL BE
A CHALLENGE.

(A) I USE B50 STRING MATERIAL, ALTHOUGH
USING THE SAME METHOD I CAN MAKE
SINEW STRINGS. FOR A BOW BETWEEN
30 AND 50 POUNDS IN DRAW WEIGHT I
USE 12 STRANDS OF B50 DIVIDED INTO
TWO BUNDLES — A TWO PLY REVERSE
TWISTED STRING.

(B) BECAUSE TWO PLYS (BUNDLES OF STRING) ARE
TIGHTLY TWISTED, THE INDIVIDUAL STRINGS
SHOULD BE CUT OFF THE ROLL, LONGER
THAN THE BOW. IT DEPENDS ON HOW
TIGHT YOU TWIST SO THERE IS NO EXACT
% I CAN GIVE YOU, BUT STRINGS CAN
BE TRIMMED OR TWISTED BACK UPON
ITSELF SO LONGER IS BETTER THAN
SHORTER.

(C) MASTER THE THEORY: TIGHTLY TWIST A
SHORT PIECE OF
STRING.

(a)

26

(b)

By holding the ends and drawing
them together you can see how
the twisted string will then double
upon itself. This twist is exactly
how short strands of natural fibers
are able to hold together when
joined to form longer strings.

(c) Though it isn't really practical to take
a single length of string, more than
twice the length of a bow and do
the same thing, we can, however
use the same twisting action starting
at one end of our bow string,
working our way to the other end.
(I am also fully able to recklessly travel
through an entire page in a single
sentence, splitting infinitives along
the way)

(d) *I consider myself daring, but I am
no daring enough to sketch human
hands. I shall replace a bad sketch
of hands from now on with a simple
icon which shows where
to pinch the working
string and where
and in which direction to pinch
twist.

87

(e) For a 64" bow, throwing in a margin of error for how tightly you will twist, along with making a tillering string for longer bows cut a length of B50, 90" long. Using that length as a guide cut 11 more to the same length and place them into two bundles. Because we shall also "plait" a loop, I suggest not having all the ends perfectly even.

NOT EVEN

Not having all the ends dead even helps them to form tapers.

(f) *Practice on short strings before going on to the actual string. Also, waxing the string plys does make it easier to work with the strings.

Before you, hanging over a closet door are two, 6 string bundles of B50, waxed, and ready to be twisted into a string. The trickiest part is the beginning, because you will be working from one end and the other ends of your

88

90" LONG PLYS WILL TANGLE AND BECOME CAT TOYS. I'VE GONE SO FAR AS STAND ON A CHAIR TO MAKE IT EASIER. WORK CAREFULLY AND KEEP THE STRING EVENLY TWISTED AS YOU WORK.

(g)

PINCH

BEGIN BY PINCHING THE TWO PLYS TOGETHER SEVERAL INCHES FROM THE END. DO NOT KNOT THE ENDS, TIE THEM TOGETHER BECAUSE WE WILL PLAIT A LOOP ON THIS END.

(h)

PINCH

WHILE PINCHING THE TWO PLYS TOGETHER WITH YOUR LEFT HAND, TWIST THE LOWER PLY TIGHTLY IN THIS DIRECTION - GOING "OVER". THEN ....

PINCH

TWIST BOTH PLYS IN THE OPPOSITE DIRECTION SO THAT TWISTED PLY IS NOW ON THE TOP.

89

(i)

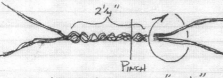

CONTINUE TO TWIST THE LOWER PLY,
AND THEN TWIST BOTH PLYS IN
THE REVERSE DIRECTION....;

UNTIL YOU HAVE 2" - 2½" OF TWISTED
BOW STRING (TILLERING STRING)

(j) PLAITING A LOOP: YOU COULD CERTAINLY
JUST TIE A KNOT ON ONE END, BUT
PLAITING LOOPS IS A GOOD TECHNIQUE
TO MASTER.

PLAITING THE LOOP IS AS SIMPLE..... AS...
MAKING A LOOP, JOIN THE SHORT ENDS
ALONG THE LONGER PLYS AND CONTINUING
TO TWIST.

90

(K) FINISHING THE ENDS:

〜〜〜〜〜〜〜〜〜〜〜〜〜〜

> YOU MAY HAVE TO TRIM THE VERY
> END OF THE STRING TO GET THEM
> TO END AT THE SAME POINT, BUT
> REALLY, ALL I EVER NEED TO DO
> IS CAREFULLY MELTING THE END
> TOGETHER WITH A LIGHTER.

12) TILLERING: SO HERE WE ARE MY
FREINDS... PAGE 91, ME SITTING HERE
WATCHING BATES MOTEL ON NETFLIX
EIGHT HOURS INTO TODAY'S WRITING
SESSION WITH MANY MORE TO GO....,
READY TO ACTUALLY AND SINCERELY
TILLER A BOW.

SOME WAYS I FEEL GUILTY. SLACKING
ACTUALLY BECAUSE THOUGH TILLERING
THE BOW IS THE GUTS OF OUR
ENDEAVOR, I CAN COME UP WITH SO
LITTLE THAT NEEDS TO BE DESCRIBED.

SINCE YOU KNOW BY NOW THAT THE
ELLIPTICAL TILLER IS THE BEND TO
SHOOT FOR, THAT IS NO MYSTERY.

BECAUSE YOU KNOW THAT REMOVING
WOOD FROM THE BELLY INCREASES THE
BEND IN THAT AREA, THAT IS ALSO NO
MYSTERY. IT'S ALSO A GIVEN THAT YOU
SHOULD WORK SLOWLY, FLEXING THE BOW
AS YOU WORK IT DOWN TO FIND IT'S TRUE
NATURE, USE THE TILLERING STICK TO
DETERMINE THE BEND, SIGHT THE BEND
FROM MANY ANGLES.... MYSTERY AFTER
MYSTERY SOLVED....

BUT YOU COULD BENEFIT FROM A BIT MORE
COACHING SO I SHALL CONTINUE....

(9) THE TILLERING STRING WORKS THE SAME
WAY AS A BOW STRING EXCEPT THAT
IT IS LONG ENOUGH TO ALLOW YOU TO
MOVE IT OUT OF THE WAY WHEN
YOU WORK THE BELLY.

AS YOU HAVE A PLAITED LOOP, IF IT IS
NOT BIG ENOUGH TO ACT AS A STANDARD
LOOP ON A STANDARD STRING, CREATE
A SLIP LOOP:

THERE ARE A NUMBER OF AUTHENTIC
NATIVE, NORTH AMERICAN KNOTS TO USE

92

ON THE OTHER END, BUT THE SIMPLEST
IS THE TIMBER HITCH. YOU WILL HAVE
EXRA LENGTH HANGING LOOSE, BUT DON'T
WORRY ABOUT IT, LET IT HANG LOOSE.

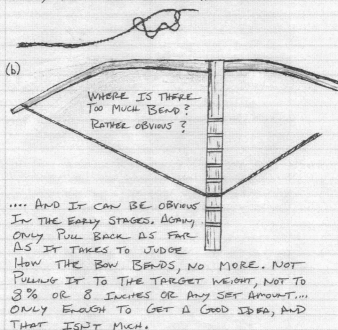

(b)

WHERE IS THERE
TOO MUCH BEND?
RATHER OBVIOUS?

.... AND IT CAN BE OBVIOUS
IN THE EARLY STAGES. AGAIN,
ONLY PULL BACK AS FAR
AS IT TAKES TO JUDGE
HOW THE BOW BENDS, NO MORE. NOT
PULLING IT TO THE TARGET WEIGHT, NOT TO
8% OR 8 INCHES OR ANY SET AMOUNT,....
ONLY ENOUGH TO GET A GOOD IDEA, AND
THAT ISN'T MUCH.

YOUR GOAL IS TOO EVEN THE BEND NOW,
NOT TO WORRY ABOUT DRAW WEIGHT.

93

(C) THERE ARE WAYS THAT CAN HELP YOU
JUDGE THE TRUE BEND, BEYOND
SIGHTING IT BY EYE FROM DIFFERENT
ANGLES.

ONE WAY IS TO SET THE BOW IN
THE TILLERING STICK WITH A MODERATE
BEND AND LAY IT DOWN ON A FLOOR
WITH EITHER SQUARES OR EVEN BOARDS.

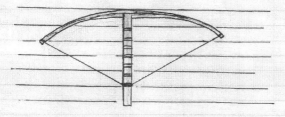

ANOTHER MORE INVOLVED WAY TO TO
DRAW AN ELLIPSE ONTO A SHEET OF ½"
PLYWOOD, OR BETTER YET, A SERIES OF
ELLIPSES FOR BOWS OF DIFFERENT LENGTHS.

94

I CAN PICTURE IT NOW: "THAT ONE" STUDENT SITTING IN THE BACK OF HIS MATH CLASS. RAISING HIS HAND, HE ASKS HIS TEACHER, " WHEN WILL WE NEED TO KNOW ABOUT ELLIPSES IN REAL LIFE?"..... "SO WE CAN MAKE BOWS"....

IF YOU ARE NOT FAMILIAR WITH THIS AMAZING SHAPE YOU SHOULD BE... THE ELLIPSE AND THE BOW FORM A UNIQUE PARTNERSHIP.

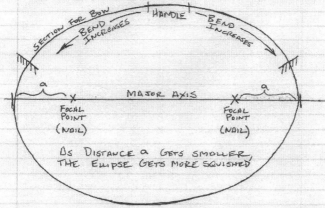

BEGINNING FROM THE HANDLE, WHERE THE BEND IS RELATIVELY FLAT, AS IT MOVES ALONG THE ARC TOWARDS THE INTERSECTION OF THE MAJOR AXIS, THE BEND "ACCELERATES".

95

OUR GOAL IS TO END OUR BOW BEFORE
IT REACHES THIS POINT, PERHAPS LEAVING
THE VERY END OF THE TIPS WITHOUT A
BEND. WE COULD BEAT OURSELVES UP
WORKING TO FIND THE EXACT POINT
WHERE THE BOW TIPS END ON OUR
ELLIPSE, BUT WE ONLY NEED TO GET
CLOSE. I SHALL GIVE YOU THE NUMBERS
FOR A 64" BOW, AND IT'S YOUR JOB
TO THINK THROUGH ADDING ELLIPTICAL
SECTIONS FOR LONGER BOWS - PROBLEM
SOLVING... THAT IS WHAT BOW MAKERS DO.

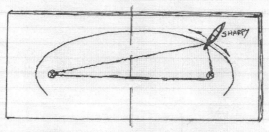

⊗ NAIL

(a) DRIVE YOUR NAILS 64" APART (THE
    FOCAL POINTS) IN YOUR PLYWOOD

(b) TAKE A LOOP OF STRING
    THAT IS 71" (THE STRING IS DOUBLED),
    AND LOOP IT OVER THE NAILS.

(c) "CATCH" THE LOOP OF STRING WITH
    A SHARPY PEN AND TRACE THE ARC.

(d) WE SHALL SAY, THAT AT THIS POINT, THE
BEND IS A PERFECT ELLIPSE. THE BOW
IS HEAVIER THAN YOUR TARGET DRAW
WEIGHT AND IT HASNT BEEN PULLED
TO IT'S FULL 26" OR 27" FOR GOOD
REASON: IT IS TOO HEAVY TO TAKE A
FULL DRAW.

WITH AN EVEN BEND THROUGHOUT BOTH
LIMBS, AND NOT SO HEAVY THAT IS WOULD
TAKE A GORILLA TO FORCE A BEND INTO
IT, IS CAN BE SAFE TO ACTUALLY BRACE
IT. WITH A SLIP LOOP, ON A STIFF
BOW, IT MAY BE HARD TO UNSTRING.
WITH A BOW THAT ISNT FINISHED, IT
IS IMPORTANT THAT A BOW CAN BE
UNSTRUNG EASILY, SO SIMPLY TAKE
YOU TILLERING STRING AND TIE A
SIMPLE KNOT WHICH FORMS A LOOP
BIG ENOUGH TO SLIDE UP AND DOWN
THE TIPS.

PRESSURE
FROM
HAND

PRESSURE
FROM
KNEE

BANDANA
GROUND ////

ONE GOOD WAY
* TO STRING A BOW
WITHOUT DAMAGING THE
LIMBS, PRESSURE SHOULD
ONLY BE APPLIED AT
THE TIPS AND CENTER
OF HANDLE (WITH YOUR
KNEE)

97

(e) STRING YOUR BOW TO A LOW BRACE
HEIGTH, 4½", PLACE IT ON THE
TILLERING STICK WITH THE STRING IN
A NOTCH THAT BENDS IT VERY SLIGHTLY.
SET THE BOW BELLY SIDE UP SO
THE BACK IS SITTING ON A FLAT
SURFACE AND MEASURE IT FROM
THE FLAT SURFACE TO EACH TIP.

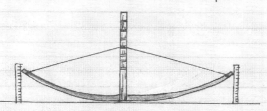

IF THE BOW WAS FINISHED AND THERE
WAS A ¼" TO ½" DIFFERENCE IN DISTANCE
WE ARE GOOD. THE STIFFER LIMB WOULD
BE THE LOWER LIMB AND I WOULD MARK
IT WITH MY BOWYERS MARK ⚡ BURNED
INTO THE BOTTOM LIMB WITH A WIRE HEATED
WITH A TORCH.

THE BOTTOM LIMB IS UNDER MORE STRESS
THAN THE UPPER LIMB SO I AS MOST OTHERS
DO, FAVOR A STIFFER LOWER LIMB. THEY
ARE ALSO USUALLY UNDER MORE STRESS DURING
STRINGING SO SOMETIMES I HAVE THE UPPER
LIMB TIED ON AND THE LOOP ON THE LOWER
TIP.   98

(f) If this is your first bow, I suggest aiming for a finished draw weight of 40 pounds at 27" with a maximum of 45 pounds. Be safe, be conservative. Some people set the bottom of the tillering stick on a bathroom scale and pull down on the string, measuring off the tillering stick how far it is drawn to reach the target weight...

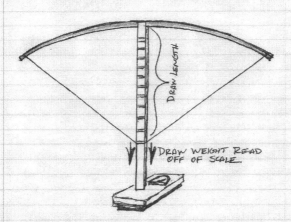

Draw Length

Draw Weight Read Off of Scale

As you work the bow down in weight, continually check the bend along with long, even strokes with 80 grit, counting each pass so the same number of passes sand each limb. Flex, sand, check...

99

FLEX, SAND, CHECK... CHECK THE TILLER,
DRAW WEIGHT...., REPEAT EACH STEP UNTIL
YOU REACH FINE TILLERING, YOUR DRAW
WEIGHT / DRAW LENGTH, AND YOU PROCLAIM
YOUR BOW READY FOR SHOOTING THAT
FIRST ARROW.

(g) I SUGGEST SHOOTING 100 ARROWS WITH
YOUR BOW AT A REDUCED DRAW.... 25", 26",
A SHORT MODIFIED DRAW THAT STILL LETS
YOU ANCHOR. I BELIEVE IT BEST THAT
YOU DON'T GO BEYOND FINE SANDING....
WORKING FROM 120, THROUGH 220, TO 400 GRIT,
AT THIS POINT BECAUSE AS YOU "SHOOT IT
IN", THE TILLERING MAY CHANGE AND
IF YOU HAVE GREASED IT, SAND PAPER
WILL CLOG UP. IF, AFTER SHOOTING IT
IN THE TILLER IS STILL GREAT YOU ARE
READY TO GREASE IT.

(h) LET'S GO OL' SCHOOL: GREASE! BACON FAT,
LARD, BEAR GREASE, MINK OIL...., GREASE.
HEAT THE BOW EITHER WITH AN ELECTRIC
RANGE OR COALS AND RUB GREASE INTO IT.
LET IT COOL, WHICH SUCKS IN GREASE
INTO IT AND WIPE IT OFF. REPEAT THIS
AFTER A DAY OR TWO, AFTER THAT GREASE
IT WHEN IT FEELS DRY. I MIX A LITTLE
BEESWAX INTO MY GREASE FOR ADDED PROTECTION.

(i) IF THIS WAS A GREEN WOOD BOW, WHY NOT START ON ANOTHER BOW FROM ANOTHER SECTION OF YOUR TREE AND LET THIS FIRST ONE CONTINUE TO CURE? IF NOT, REMEMBER TO BRACE TO THE MINIMUM, 5½" TO LIMIT STRESS ON THE BOW. THANK YOU, AND ALL THE BEST AS YOU CONTINUE ON TO BOW #2, THE RAWHIDE BACKED LONGBOW.

CHAPTER 5

PROJECT BOW #2

RED OAK LONGBOW

"THE TIME TRAVELER"

TIME TRAVELER? HUH? THIS IS AN "AMERICAN STYLE LONGBOW", RIGHT? NAW, THE CONCEPT OF A LONG, FLAT OR FLATTISH BELLIED BOW WITH A NARROW DEEP HANDLE HAS BEEN FLOATING AROUND EUROPE FOR MANY THOUSANDS OF YEARS. IT IS A GREAT DESIGN SO IF PEOPLE WANT TO GIVE US CREDIT FOR IT, THAT'S A WONDERFUL THING. BUT BY DOING THAT WE TAKE AWAY FROM THE PEOPLE THAT ACTUALLY DESIGNED THESE CREATURES.

＊TANGENT ALERT: I WONDER IF THE STELLMOOR BOW FRAGMENTS FOUND IN GERMANY WERE ACTUALLY MADE FROM THE HEARTWOOD OF SCOTS PINE.... OR WERE THEY MADE FROM DENSE LIMBS? I THINK I ALREADY BROUGHT THAT UP....

IN THIS SECTION WE WILL MAKE OUR BOW FROM A RED OAK BOARD, 3/4" THICK. THE RISER NEEDS TO BE BUILT UP SO A BLOCK MUST BE GLUED TO THE CENTER SECTION. IF YOU MEASURE MY FULL SIZED HANDLE, SIDE PROFILE, YOU WILL SEE THAT THE BLOCK IS THICKER THAN 3/4". THIS WOULD BE A GOOD OPPORTUNITY TO ADD A THIN STRIP OF A DIFFERENT COLORED WOOD BETWEEN

102

Two RED oak BLOCKS TO ADD A FLASHY BIT OF STYLE. I SUGGEST USING GORILLA GLUE TO JOIN THESE BITS AND PARTS INTO ONE UNIT. GORILLA GLUE EXPANDS IT'S WAY INTO THE DEPTHS OF THE WOOD CREATING A MASSIVE BOND. GIVE IT A TRY, IT WORKS.

THE THEORY OF THIS BOW MIRRORS THE PHILOSOPHY OF THE MEARE HEATH BOW: BIG, "OVER BUILT" MEANING BEEFY ENOUGH TO TAKE LONG DRAWS AND HIGHER WEIGHTS WITH A SAFETY MARGIN, AND BLESSED WITH SIMPLE RELIABILITY. MY MEASUREMENTS FOR THIS BOW WAS TAKEN FROM A BOW I MAKE AND SELL CALLED MY "SNAKE BOW". I CALL IT A SNAKE BOW BECAUSE MY TEMPLATES OUTLINE A SNAKEY LINE, MIMICKING A BOW MADE FROM A WONKEY NATURAL STAVE. WHEN I BACK MY SNAKE BOWS WITH FABRIC STRIPS DECORATED WITH SNAKE SKIN PATTERNS (WHICH I BUY FROM MY FAVORITE PRIMITIVE ARCHERY SUPPLIER), THEY LOOK AMAZING. WHEN BACKED WITH CLOTH, OR WITH RAWHIDE WHICH WE WILL DO HERE, THESE 2" WIDE, 70" LONG BOWS ARE BULLET PROOF: 30" DRAWS AND 50 PLUS POUND DRAW

103

WEIGHTS ARE VERY POSSIBLE IN RED OAK.
AT LESSER DRAW WEIGHTS AND SHORTER
DRAW LENGTHS THEY ARE EVEN FARTHER
AWAY FROM THEIR BREAKING POINT....
THINK OF CRAMMING A BIG ENGINE INTO
A SMALL CAR. THAT ENGINE WOULD
NOT BE STRAINING TO PUSH THAT LIGHT
WEIGHT AROUND THE BLOCK. BUT ENOUGH
OF THAT, LET'S TALK ABOUT BOARDS.

1) <u>WUD FROM TREES:</u> WITH STAVE MADE
BOWS WE TEND TO GET FEWER BOWS
FROM OR "LOGS" THAN SAW LOGS CUT
BY MILLS CAN PRODUCE. ONE SIMPLE
REASON IS THAT OUR LOGS ARE USUALLY
SMALLER. THE OTHER REASON IS THAT
WITH BOARD BOWS WE HAVE A WIDER
CHOICE OF GRAIN PATTERNS:

(A) LET'S BEGIN WITH A LIVE SAWN
       LOG..,

17" DIA
TREE CUT
INTO 1"
BOARDS

104

ALTHOUGH MY DRAWING OF THIS 17" DIAMETER
LOG, LIVE SAWN INTO 1" BOARDS IS A
PSYCHEDELIC NIGHTMARE (DON'T STARE AT
IT TOO LONG), IF WE TAKE IT APART AND
ENVISION HOW MANY OF THE BOARDS HAVE
WORKABLE RIFT SAWN GRAIN, WE CAN
FIND MANY BOWS HIDDEN IN THERE....

RIFT SAWN BOARDS (BOW WOOD)

(a)   (b)   (c)

MOST OF THE BOARDS WE WOULD THINK OF
AS RIFT SAWN HOVER AROUND 45°, BUT
THEY ACTUALLY TYPICALLY RANGE BETWEEN
30° AND 60°. I FAVOR BOARDS WITH
LOWER ANGLES SUCH AS EXAMPLE (a),
BUT A HIGHER 45° LIKE EXAMPLE (b)
IS PERFECTLY GOOD FOR SELF BOWS.
EXAMPLE (c) IS GETTING PRETTY CLOSE TO
QUARTER SAWN. I WOULD USE HIGHER
ANGLES FOR BACKED WIDE BOWS OR
NARROW SELF BOWS. ON WIDER BOWS,
EVEN STRAIGHT GRAINED BOARDS WILL
"RUN OFF" ALONG THE EDGES. LET ME
EXPLAIN:

105

THE END GRAIN FOLLOWS THE PATTERN
ON THE FACE OF THE BOARD. THE
WIDER THE LINES ON THE FACE OF THE
BOARD, THE LOWER THE ANGLE —

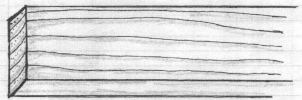

(a) HIGH ANGLE RINGS APPROACHING QUARTER SAWN

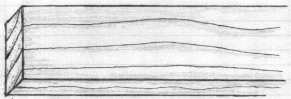

(b) MID ANGLE AROUND 45°

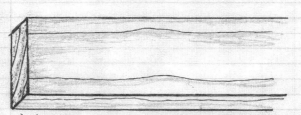

c) LOWER ANGLES APPROACHING FLAT SAWN

a) HIGH ANGLE RINGS CAN EASILY RUN
   OFF OF THE EDGES OF A WIDE BOW
   CAUSING ISSUES IF THE BOW ISN'T
   BACKED. THE INTERESTING THING IS
   THAT HICKORY STRIPS THAT ARE USED
   IN BACKING BOWS IS IN MANY CASES
   QUARTER SAWN. I BELIVE THAT IT IS
   EFFECTIVE BECAUSE IT IS USED IN THIN
   STRIPS HELD TO THE BOW WITH A STRONG
   GLUE HELPING TO KEEP IT FROM
   SPLITTING ALONG THE GROWTH RINGS.
   HICKORY ALSO HAS A GRAIN THAT HOLDS
   TOGETHER BETTER THAN OTHER WOODS.
   HICKORY BACKING IS ALSO TYPICALLY USED
   ON NARROW BOWS WHICH DON'T HAVE
   EXTREME CHANGES IN WIDTH, CAUSING
   ISSUES WITH GROWTH RINGS RUNNING
   OFF EDGES ALONG THE LIMBS.

b) MID ANGLE GROWTH RINGS HAVE MORE
   AREA BETWEEN GROWTH RINGS IN A
   BOW'S LIMB. HAVING MORE SURFACE AREA
   FOR A WOOD WITHOUT INTERLOCKING
   GRAIN HELPS HOLD THE BOW TOGETHER.

c) LOWER ANGLES HAVE EVEN MOR SURFACE
   AREA BETWEEN RINGS ALONG WITH
   ALLOWING A WIDER BOW WITH BIGGER
   CHANGES OF WIDTH BETTER OPPORTUNITY TO
   BE ORIENTED WITHOUT "RUN OUT" ALONG THE LIMBS.

107

To sum up the task of choosing a board: 1) Look for boards with lines that run in straight lines on the face, from end to end 2) Begin at the upper angle of 45° and lower angle of 30° for wider bows (2" plus), and for narrower bows go up to 60°.

Not all boards should be ignored if they are plain sawn or quarter sawn:

Plain, or flat sawn boards may possibly be fine to use provided that they follow, or very closely follow the rings. Backing a bow helps even further if there isnt a perfectly followed growth ring. * If you are brand new to bow building, stay with rift sawn. The perfect situation is the board which allows you to follow, or work down to a single growth rings. An allowable board is one that has a run-off of growth rings in an area in the center on a stiff handled bow, or maybe near the tips. I would suggest backing if there is any run-off.

108

NOT ALL QUARTER SAWN BOARDS ARE
ALIKE. IF YOU ARE LOCATED IN AN AREA
WHICH HAS ACCESS TO SAW MILLS OR
WHERE ONE CAN BUY BOAT BUILDING
MATERIALS, YOU ARE IN LUCK. MANY
SMALL SAWMILLS CAN SELL CUSTOM
BOARDS - BOARDS THAT YOU CAN AIR
DRY. IN WHAT EVER DIMENSION OR GRAIN
ORIENTATION YOU WISH. PICTURE HOW
MANY "GROWTH RING" BOWS AWAIT,
HIDING IN A 3" WIDE, QUARTER
SAWN BOARD CUT FROM THE CENTER
OF A TREE.' BETTER YET, BUY A SAW
LOG AND TRACK DOWN SOMEONE WITH
A WOODMIZER BAND SAW....

IN EACH OF
THESE SECTIONS
THERE ARE
NUMEROUS
GROWTH RING BOWS

BEING GREEN,
YOU HAVE CONTROL
OF THEIR CURING.

MILLS AND LUMBER SUPPLIERS ALSO
OFFER WHITE OAK AND ASH IN QUARTER
SAWN LUMBER. ANOTHER POSSIBLE SOURCE
ARE MILLS THAT SUPPLY WHITE OAK
FOR WHISKEY BARREL STAVES. THEY
UNDERSTAND HOW TO CUT CLEAN STAVES
IN AN ORIENTATION SIMILAR TO OUR NEEDS.

109

2) MARK THE CENTERS OF YOUR RISER BLOCK(S)
AND BOW, WIPE A DAMP CLOTH ON ONE SURFACE,
APPLY A THIN EVEN LAYER OF GORILLA GLUE
ON THE OTHER SURFACE AND CLAMP THEM
TIGHTLY TOGETHER. IF YOU USE C CLAMPS
CUSION THE BACK OF THE BOW WITH THIN
STRIPS OF WOOD TO PROTECT THE BACK FROM
CLAMP MARKS. YOU CAN REALLY CLAMP DOWN
ON A GORILLA GLUE JOINT. DRY JOINTS
ARE LESS THAN A PROBLEM THAN WITH
OTHER GLUES. ALLOW THE GLUE TO CURE
OVER NIGHT.

3) AS WITH ANY OTHER BOW, USE A
STRING TO MARK THE TRUE CENTER OF
THE TIPS AND CENTER OF THE HANDLE.

4) USING MY MEASUREMENTS, LAY OUT
YOUR BOW'S FACE. YOU CAN TRACE THE
FULL SIZED DRAWINGS AND TRANSFER
THEM TO POSTER BOARD. THE TRUE
MEASUREMENT IS WITHIN THE LINES —
CUT THEM SO THE LINES ARE REMOVED
OR SPLIT. * IF A GLUED ON RISER BLOCK
IS IN ANY WAY IN AN AREA OF BEND,
YOU RISK THE BLOCK SEPARATING ON IT'S
LEADING EDGE. MY BOW HAS A BLOCK THAT
ENDS BEFORE ANY BENDING OCCURS SO
WE ARE SAFE.

110

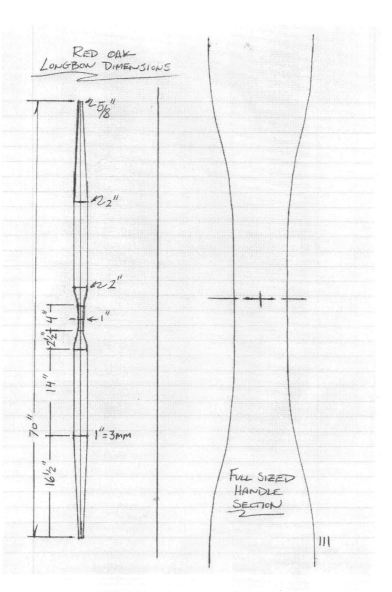

RED OAK
LONGBOW DIMENSIONS

2-5/8"

⌀2"

⌀2"

1"

4"

2½"

14"

70"

1" = 3mm

16½"

FULL SIZED
HANDLE
SECTION

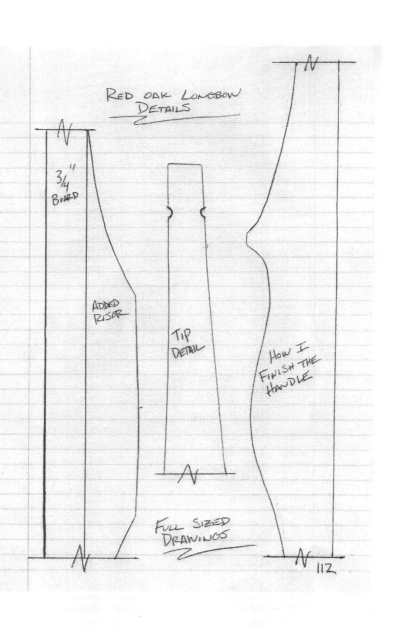

Red Oak Longbow
Details

3/4" Board

Added Riser

Tip Detail

How I Finish the Handle

Full Sized Drawings

112

5) EVEN THOUGH THE TABLE SAW DID QUITE
A BIT OF WORK FOR YOU, YOU STILL HAVE
THE TAPER OF THE TIPS AND THE HANDLE
SECTION TO WORK. AS WITH ANY BOW,
YOU WILL HAVE AN EASIER TIME FINE
TUNING TO YOUR LINES AFTER YOU DO
SOME THINNING OF THE BOW. I ALWAYS
SUGGEST ROUGHING THE FACE TO WITHIN
AN EIGHTH OR LESS, OF AN INCH OF YOUR
LINES AND ZERO IN AFTER YOUR FIRST
ROUND OF THINNING.

   A TECHNIQUE I USE TO ROUGH OUT A
THICK HANDLE SECTION IS TO SAW CLOSE
TO THE LINES WITH A GOOD MARGIN FOR
SAFETY IN THIS WAY:

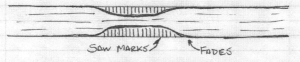

SAW MARKS   FADES

   STARTING AT THE FADE, JAM A KNIFE
INTO THE CUTS, ROTATING THE KNIFE TOWARD
THE HANDLE CENTER TO CHIP OUT THE
BLOCKS, WHILE AVOIDING SPLITING INTO THE
BOW'S FADES. THIS WILL LEAVE A ROUGH,
STEPPED SURFACE BUT IT REMOVES WOOD
QUICKLY. I ALSO WILL USE THIS TECHNIQUE
TO THIN LIMBS ON STAVE BOWS ON RARE
OCCASIONS... WITH REALLY TOUGH, HARD WOODS.

6) THINNING. I REALLY ENJOY THE FEELING OF THESE BOWS WHEN THEY ARE ELLIPTICALLY TILLERED: HAVING A SMOOTH BEND THROUGH THE TIPS HELPS REDUCE STRING FOLLOW. IT ALSO MAKES A SMOOTH FAST BOW BY MINIMIZING THE AMOUNT OF MASS THOSE LONG LIMBS HAVE TO MOVE. THIS BRINGS ME TO THE DISCUSSION OF RAWHIDE BACKING:

RAWHIDE BACKING GIVE PROTECTION FROM EXPLODING BACKS. THE TRADE OFF IS ADDED WEIGHT. IF YOUR GOAL IS A BOW UNDER 45 POUNDS, THIS LONG AND WIDE CONSIDER NOT RAWHIDE BACKING. IF YOU WISH TO INCREASE DRAW WEIGHT OR EXTEND THE DRAW LENGTH TO 30" PLUS, OR BOTH, GO AHEAD AND BACK IT. I SHOULD ADD, THOUGH, IF YOU WANT A "BULLET PROOF" BOW AND DON'T MIND LOWERING ARROW CAST SLIGHTLY, OR WISH TO REFLEX THE BOW WITH DRY HEAT OR STEAM, OR ADD RECURVES, THEN BACKING A LIGHTER BOW MAKES SENSE. IF YOU WISH TO PAINT YOUR BOW RAWHIDE BACKING IS ALSO HELPFULL. IT'S A CHOICE WITH SOME TRADE OFFS.

BACK TO THINNING — WE SHALL BE CONSERVATIVE WHEN WE SCRIBE THIS BOW. MORE SO THEN WE WERE WHEN WE SCRIBED THE

THICKNESS ON OUR D BOW. THE LIMBS ARE
LONGER AND WE HAVE A STIFF HANDLE
SO WE WILL RELY MORE ON OUR TILLERING
STICK THAN ATTEMPTING TO GET CLOSE
RIGHT AWAY. WE SHALL SCRIBE A LINE
5/8" OF AN INCH ON EACH SIDE OF EACH
LIMB, STOPPING AT A POINT, 8" FROM THE
BOW'S CENTER. IF YOU MEASURE THE
THICKNESS OF THE HANDLE TEMPLATE,
IT REDUCES TO 3/4", THE THICKNESS
OF THE BOARD. I CONSIDER THIS, THE
AREA WHERE LONGBOW MAKERS HAVE
TO USE CAUTION: IT IS TOO EASY TO
OVERWORK THE AREA NEAR THE FADES.

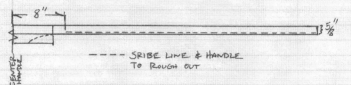

SRIBE LINE & HANDLE
TO ROUGH OUT

CENTER HANDLE

8"

5/8"

AFTER ROUGHING OUT THE BOW TO THESE
LINES YOU COULD GO A BIT FARTHER: SCRIBE
A 1/2" LINE 14" FROM THE TIPS AND WORK
THE TIP THICKESS TO THIS NEXT LEVEL.

TIP

3 1/2"

14"

115

7) ROUNDING THE BACK: I LIKE TO MIMIC
THE ORGANIC SHAPE OF A NATURAL
STAVE MADE BOW WHEN I MAKE A
BOARD BOW. IT ISNT SO MUCH AS A
WAY TO FOOL PEOPLE INTO THINKING
THAT IT IS SOMETHING THAT IT IS NOT...
IT IS BECAUSE FOLLOWING THE SHAPES
IN NATURE GIVE RATIO AND PROPORTIONS
THAT GO BEYOND PLEASING, THE FORM
A FUNCTIONALITY THAT WE SOMETIMES
OVERLOOK... THE GOLDEN RATIO, FIBONACCI
NUMBER.... FOLLOW THE PATTERNS. TH
SHOULD HAVE BEEN A TANGENT ALERT!

PICTURE A SECTION OF TREE IN WHICH
WE SHALL WORK INTO A BOW:

IF WE LOOK STRAIGHT DOWN AT THIS PIECE
OF TREE, AND PLACE A BOW'S OUTLINE
ONTO IT, SOMETHING BECOMES APPARENT:
THE WIDER THE BOW, THE GREATER THE
CURVE. IN NARROW AREAS SUCH AS TIPS,
IT IS ALMOST FLAT. IN PARALLEL
D BOWS IT IS ALMOST CONSTANT :

116

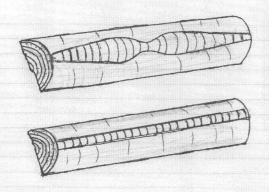

ONE OF EASIER WAYS TO GET A NATURAL
SHAPE IS TO ROUND THE BACK BEFORE
TAPERING THE BLANK INTO THE FINISHED
FACE SHAPE. IT'S ALSO PRETTY EASY
TO SCRIBE THE LINES FOR THE BEVEL
(REFER TO THE D BOW SECTION) UP
UNTIL THE TAPER AND THEN USING A
STRAIGHT EDGE, CONTINUE THEM OFF
THE TAPER!

WOW, I ACTUALLY FORGOT TO SAY THAT THIS
IS THE TIME TO BEVEL AND ROUND
THE BACK OF THE BOW!

I'VE FULLY ROUNDED THE BACKS OF MY
BOWS -

(BOARD BOW)

STOPPED AT JUST ROUNDING EDGES ~

(BOARD BOW)

DECROWNED NATURAL TREE STAVES
WHEN THE CROWN IS TOO HIGH.... WHEN
MAKING WIDER BOWS OUT OF SMALL
TREES -

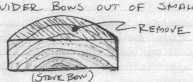
← REMOVE

(STAVE BOW)

.... AND LEFT THE CROWN INTACT ....'

WITH MOST OF MY BOARD BOWS I
MOST OFTEN LEAVE THE CENTER LINE OF
THE BACK FLAT, ROUNDING IT ALONG
THE EDGES AS A' GOOD COMPROMISE
BETWEEN STYLE
AND FUNCTION.

FLAT

(BOARD BOW)

118

8) OF TILLERING AND BACKING :

QUESTION : JOHN, DO YOU TILLER THE
BOW BEFORE YOU BACK IT, OR
BACK IT BEFORE YOU TILLER IT?
ANSWER : YES.

A BIG PART OF BOW MAKING IS
PROBLEM SOLVING AND BECAUSE EACH
BOW IS AN INDIVIDUAL, EACH BOW PRESENTS
US WITH DIFFERENT WAYS TO SOLVE
THESE "PROBLEMS". TYPICALLY, I WORK
THE BOW TO THE POINT OF TILLERING
BEFORE I BACK IT, BUT NOT TO THE
POINT OF IT BEING FINISHED TO IT'S
DESIRED WEIGHT... BACKING WILL CHANGE
THE BOW'S DRAW WEIGHT SO THAT
POINT IS OBVIOUS.

I DO QUITE A BIT OF TILLERING
THOUGH FOR SEVERAL REASONS:
(a) THERE IS A POSSIBILTY THAT THE
BACKING COULD BE DAMAGED DURING
TILLERING SO I LIMIT POTENTIAL
DAMGE BY LIMITING EXPOSURE.
(b) WITH SINEW, AND RAWHIDE TO SOME
DEGREE, ON AN ALMOST FINISHED BOW,
THE BACKING CAN SHRINK AND PULL
THE BOW INTO REFLEX. A THICKER
BOW MAY STOP THAT AND BE "STUNTED,"

(c) I SHAPE MANY OF MY BACKED BOWS
EITHER BY RECURVING OR SHAPING
INTO GULL WINGS AND THIN WOOD
IS MORE EASILY SHAPED THAN THICK
WOOD.

9) <u>ROUGH TILLERING</u>: BY ROUGH, I AM
IN NO MEANS REFERRING TO BAD
TILLERING. IN MY MIND, A PIECE OF
WUD THAT HAS A HINGE-y BEND OR
AN UNEVEN, UGLY BEND IS <u>NOT</u>
TILLERED. SOOO.... TO EVEN BE CONSIDERED
AS ROUGHLY TILLERED, THE BEND MUST
BE EVEN, WELL DISTRIBUTED, AND
CLOSE TO FINAL TILLERING AND FINAL
DRAW WEIGHT / LENGTH.

    I AM AT THIS POINT DEBATING HOW
DEEP TO GET INTO TILLERING. I COVERED
TILLERING; THE HOW TO'S AND WHY'S IN
THE CHAPTER ON THE D BOW, SO A
LOT OF INFORMATION IS ALREADY HERE.
I WILL THOUGH, MAKE EVERY ATTEMPT TO
ADD SPECIFIC TID BITS THAT WILL HELP
YOU TILLER A STIFF HANDLED LONG BOW.

    I HAVE ALREADY MENTIONED DIFFERENT
FORMS OF TILLER, AND THEY CAN AND
DO HAVE SOME ADVANTAGES:

120

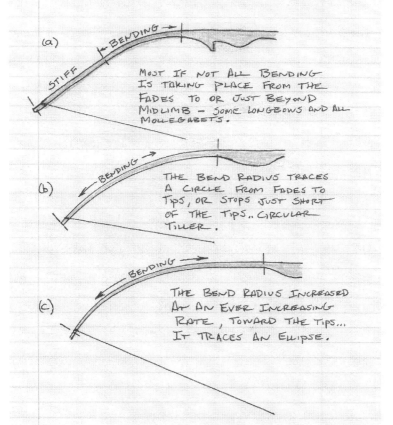

(a)

BENDING →

STIFF

MOST IF NOT ALL BENDING
IS TAKING PLACE FROM THE
FADES TO OR JUST BEYOND
MIDLIMB — SOME LONGBOWS AND ALL
MOLLEGABETS.

(b)

BENDING →

THE BEND RADIUS TRACES
A CIRCLE FROM FADES TO
TIPS, OR STOPS JUST SHORT
OF THE TIPS.. CIRCULAR
TILLER.

(c)

BENDING →

THE BEND RADIUS INCREASED
AT AN EVER INCREASING
RATE, TOWARD THE TIPS...
IT TRACES AN ELLIPSE.

121

FIGURE (a) CAN BE DECEPTIVE BECAUSE WATCHING A REFLEX DEFLEX BOW WILL RESEMBLE THIS BEND EVEN THOUGH THERE IS ACTUAL, REAL BENDING TAKING PLACE BEYOND THE APPARENT END OF THE BENDING.... IT'S A TRICK OF THE EYE.

WE DO THOUGH SEE SELF LONGBOWS WITH BEND ENDING WELL SHORT OF THE TIPS. SHOULD I SPEAK ILL OF THIS BRAND OF TILLER? NOPE, BECAUSE IT IS NECESSARY IN THE CASE OF MOLLEGABETS, ALLOWABLE FOR BOWS MADE OF OSAGE AND OTHER MMA LEVEL WOODS, AND THEORETICALLY A FAST TILLER FOR SOME DESIGNS.

FOR OUR PROJECT BOW, BECAUSE OF THE MATERIAL AND FACE PROFILE, I DO NOT SUGGEST LIMITING THE BEND TO THIS DEGREE.

FIGURE (b) I LIKE CIRCULAR TILLER. IT DISTRIBUTES BEND OVER A LONG AREA, IT'S PRETTY, AND WITH PYRAMID BOWS WITH THEIR CONSTANT THICKNESS, A NATURAL CONSEQUENCE. IT'S SEEN IN ENGLISH LONGBOWS, AND IF YOU REACH CIRCULAR TILLERING WITH YOUR PROJECT BOW, GOOD JOB!

FIGURE (c) I FAVOR ELLIPTICAL TILLER IN
NARROW D BOWS AS WELL AS STIFF
HANDLE LONGBOWS (NOT INCLUDING
MOLLEGABETS). THIS IS A PERSONAL LIFE
CHOICE ON MY PART. IT IS NOT TO SAY
"IT IS THE BEST AND ALL OTHERS ARE
STINKERS", TO SOME DEGREE, OTHER
TILLERS ARE JUST AS EFFECTIVE IF THE
BOWS ARE NOT BUMPING UP AGAINST THEIR
LIMITS. I DO SUGGEST WORKING TOWARD
AN ELLIPTICAL TILLER WITH THE BEND
ENDING WITHIN SIX OR SO INCHES FROM
THE TIPS, BECAUSE IT WORKS WELL ALONG
WITH FIGHTING STRING FOLLOW.

10) <u>ROUGH TILLERING - WORKING</u>: * IF YOUR
GOAL IS TO RAWHIDE BACK YOUR BOW,
YOU MAY AS WELL TILLER CLOSE TO TARGET
DRAW WEIGHT TO WITHIN SEVERAL
INCHES SHORT OF YOUR TARGET DRAW
LENGTH IF <u>THIS</u> RED OAK BOARD BOW
WILL BE OVER 50 POUNDS. IF YOU ARE
AIMING FOR LESS THAN 50 POUNDS, YOU MAY
COMPLETE THE TILLERING PROCESS BEFORE
BACKING, AND GO BACK AFTER THE
BACKING DRIES AND FINE TUNE THE
TILLER... IT WILL CHANGE SLIGHTLY.

123

CARE. OF COURSE EVERY PART OF THE BOW
REQUIRES CARE, BE AFRAID, VERY VERY
AFRAID OF THIS AREA. WELL, NOT SO MUCH,
BUT TREAT THIS AREA LAST, AND YES,
WITH CAUTION. THE CENTER OF THE BOW
IS THE CENTER OF LEVERAGE, SO REMOVING
WOOD IN THE CENTER OR NEAR THE
CENTER CARRIES GREAT RISKS.

* THE FIRST STEP IS TO CONCENTRATE
ON ACHEIVING YOUR DESIRED TILLER UP
TO THE 8" FROM CENTER LINE. DRAW
WEIGHT IS NOT AN ISSUE YET - 50 POUNDS,
45 POUNDS, 30 POUNDS AT 10 INCHES OF
DRAW AT THIS POINT IS OK. ARRIVE AT
A PRETTY BEND THAT IS EVEN IN
BOTH LIMBS IS THE GOAL. IT LIMITS
THE DEGREE THAT YOU ARE STRESSING
LESSER AREAS ALONG YOUR LIMBS ALONG
WITH MAKING REDUCING THE WEIGHT
A MUCH SIMPLER PROCESS.

* ONCE THE LIMBS ARE BALANCED AND
THE SHAPE OF THE FINAL TILLER SHAPE
(UP TO THE 8" POINT), CLAMP YOUR BOW
BACKSIDE DOWN ON A WORK SURFACE,
LOAD THAT SANDING BLOCK WITH 80
GRIT, AND COUNT AS YOU SAND THE
FULL LENGTH OF EACH LIMB 20 TIMES.

124

20 IS JUST A NUMBER. IT COULD BE
10, 15, 20, 27.... THE IMPORTANT POINT
IS THAT THE SANDING STROKES ARE
EVEN, FULL LIMB, AND GIVEN EQUAL
PRESSURE. FOLLOW THIS WITH CHECKING
YOUR PROGRESS ON THE TILLERING TREE
(OR STICK), FOLLOWED BY MORE SANDING.

* THIS NEXT STEP IS A MILESTONE:
WHEN YOU CAN JUDGE THAT THE LIMBS
ARE EVEN AND THE WEIGHT HAS BEEN
REDUCED TO HITTING YOUR DESIRED DRAW
WEIGHT AT ABOUT HALF OF YOUR DESIRED
DRAW LENGTH, STRING YOUR BOW TO LOW
BRACE. THIS BOW CAN BE BRACED TO 6½
TO 7", SO BY LOW BRACE I AM REFERRING
TO 4 OR 5" INCHES. AT THE SLIGHTEST
HINT THAT THE LIMBS ARE UNEVEN UNSTRING
IT AT ONCE AND EVENLY SAND THE
STIFFER LIMB UNTIL YOU CAN STRING IT
TO LOW BRACE AND HAVE EVEN LIMBS.

* THIS IS THE POINT WHERE YOU CAN WORK
THE BEND TOWARDS THE FADES. DO NOT
WORK A BEND RIGHT INTO THE FADES,
MAINTAIN A GRACE ZONE, BUT DO GET A
FINISHED BEND NOW, BEFORE WORKING
TOWARD YOUR TARGET DRAW WEIGHT/LENGTH.

125

* You are now at the point of reducing
the draw weight to the point of personal
preference. When I make a bow for
me, measuring the actual weight on a
scale is neither here nor there.
My goal is to make a bow that feels
good and numbers take a back seat.
I'm going to close this section by
saying to use a combination of sighting
from every angle, hold the handle
near your chest, drawing (flexing)
the bow by pulling from the side
and sight down the lower (flip the
bow, sight, flip the bow, sight) limb
to see how it bends... sand the limbs
and count.... tillering stick.... repeat
the steps.... "whew".... keep going
until it's a bow.

* If you are not going to back it, follow
the same procedures as with the D bow:
finish sand it, refine the tips and
handle, but wait to grease it or add
another type of finish until you've fired
a number of arrows and taken some
days of stringing to judge the true
tillering.

126

11) Refining the Handle:

My Templates Give You Two Options:
A Symmetrical Handle:

And An Asymmetrica Handle:

With a Symmetrical Handle On a Bow
With Equal Length Limbs, We Have
The Advantage of Switching the Upper
Limb With The Lower Limb If The Limbs
Shift Balance: The Lower Limb Is
Under Greater Stress When Shooting
And Stringing, So It Is possible over
Time For The Upper Limb To Become
The Stiffer Limb. Symmetrical Handles
Allow Us To Flip The Bow.

127

WITH A ASYMMETRICAL HANDLE, WE HAVE THE ADVANTAGE OF WORKING THE HAND GRIP TO BETTER FIT YOUR HAND. THE ADDED FLAIR ON MY TEMPLATE REALLY MAKES THIS HANDLE SHAPE LOOK BEAUTIFUL. WE ARE BOUND TO A DEFINITE UPPER LIMB AND DEFINITE LOWER LIMB SO I SUGGEST ADDING THIS STEP TO HELP KEEP THEM BALANCED LONGER: STRING THEM UPSIDE DOWN. IN THE CASE OF BOWS WHICH HAVE THE STRING TIED TO ONE TIP WITH A LOOP ON THE OTHER, KEEP THE LOOP ON THE LOWER LIMB.

12) RAWHIDE BACKING: PLEASE KNOW THAT BACKING A BOW WITH RAWHIDE IS NOT MYSTERIOUS OR DIFFICULT. IF YOU BUY MATCHED STRIP FROM A GOOD PRIMITIVE ARCHERY SUPPLY COMPANY, THE PREPARATION REQUIRED OF YOU IS MINIMAL. I DO SUGGEST DEGREASING THEM DURING THE SOAKING PROCESS, BUT THAT IS ABOUT IT. I BUY THEM CLEAN AND SANDED AND READY TO APPLY. HOW I WILL WORK THROUGH THIS SECTION IS FROM THE POINT OF THE HIDE BEING TAKEN OFF OF A DEER. STEP IN AT THE

128

POINT TO WHICH YOUR HIDES ARE PREPARED.

(a) EVEN IF YOU DO A "CLEAN SKIN", THERE WILL BE STRIPS OF MEAT, FAT, AND THE HAIR ON THE HIDE WHICH ALL HAVE TO BE REMOVED. IF YOU CAN'T WORK THE HIDE RIGHT AWAY YOU CAN SPRAD IT OUT IN THE SUN TO DRY OR IF YOU ARE IN A MORE HUMID ENVIRONMENT SOAK IT IN A SALT BRINE AND LET IT DRY.

(b) THERE ARE DIFFERENT WAYS IN WHICH TO REMOVE DEER HAIR: ONE I CALL STINKING THE HIDE AND THE OTHER TWO REQUIRE SOAKING IN A SOLUTION TO CAUSE HAIR SLIP.

    * THE STINK METHOD: THIS RELIES ON THE HIDE TO BEGIN ROTTING TO ALLOW THE HAIR TO SLIP. IT CAN EITHER BE BURIED, ROLLED INTO A TARP WHILE WET, OR ALLOWED TO SOAK IN A TUB UNTIL IT TURNS INTO A PETRI DISH. MONITOR THE HIDE SO IT DOESN'T ROT TOO MUCH AND WHEN IT'S TIME, THE HAIR CAN BE SCRAPED OFF IN STINKY CHUNKS. NOT A PLEASANT METHOD BUT IT WORKS, REQUIRING A LOT OF RINSING, WASHING,

129

AND SUNSHINE TO RELIEVE THE SMELL.

* SOAKING IN AN ASH SOLUTION: HARD WOOD ASHES IN WATER FORM AN ALKALINE SOLUTION THAT CAN CAUSE HAIR SLIP. THERE ARE SEVERAL WAYS TO DO THIS, BUT BASICALLY IT IS NOTHING MORE THAN SOAKING HIDES IN A SLURRY OF OAK ASHES AND WATER, AND WAITING.

* SOAKING IN LIME. USE CAUTION WHEN WORKING WITH LIME — IN OPEN AIR, SAFETY GLASSES, LONG SLEEVE SHIRT, RUBBER GLOVES, ETC. LIME CAN BURN!! IN A PLASTIC TUB, ADD ENOUGH WATER TO FULLY IMMERSE THE HIDE. ADD A GOOD AMOUNT OF LIME, STIR, AND DUNK THE HIDE PLACING A ROCK ON TOP TO KEEP IT DOWN. PERHAPS SPRINKLE MORE LIME OVER IT. WAIT 24 HOURS AND TEST FOR HAIR SLIPPAGE. IF IT COMES OFF EASILY, IT IS READY TO PULL AND SCRAPE OFF THE HAIR. IF NOT, WAIT UNTIL THE NEXT MORNING. MOST OF THE TIME SOME HAIR WILL BE STUBBORN. LEAVING TRACES OF HAIR IS BETTER THAN "OVER LIMING" HIDES SO RINSE AND WASH, AND PREPARE FOR THE NEXT STEP...

130

(C) EITHER ON A DRYING FRAME OR BY
SIMPLY NAILING YOUR HIDE TO A BOARD
OR SIDE OF A SHED FLESH SIDE OUT,
ALLOW YOUR HIDE TO DRY. AN INTERESTING
THING HAPPENS WHETHER IT IS A DEER
HIDE OR COWHIDE... A LOT OF THE
REMAINING FLESH AND FAT CAN PEEL OFF
BY JUST USING YOUR FINGERS. IT MAY
ALSO TAKE SCRAPING AND SANDING (ORBITAL
DISC SANDERS ARE SOOO NICE), BUT IT
ISN'T ROCKET SURGERY. CLEAN YOUR
HIDE.

(D) CONVERTING THE HIDE INTO RAWHIDE
HAS BEEN COMPLETED. YOU NOW HAVE
MATERIAL FOR DRUM HEADS, SNOW SHOES,
LASHINGS FOR DOG SLEDS (BEEN THERE),
OR BOW BACKING. RAWHIDE HAS A
GRAIN, LIKE WOOD HAS A GRAIN (IN SOME
WAYS). A GOOD ORIENTATION FOR BOW
BACKING IS.....

FRONT TO BACK.
NOT ONLY BECAUSE
OF LENGTH, BUT
BECAUSE OF THICKNESS
AND STRENGTH.

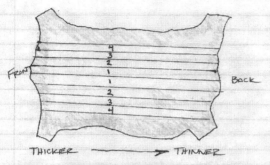

THICKER ———————→ THINNER

WITH A SHORT BOW, EACH OF THESE
SECTIONS COULD POSSIBLY REACH FROM TIP
TO TIP. A LONGER BOW WILL REQUIRE TWO
MATCHED STRIPS. * IF THE HIDE IS
LONG ENOUGH, REDUCE YOUR WASTE BY
CUTTING YOUR STRIPS SHORTER THAN THE
LENGTH OF THE HIDE –

HIDES ARE THICKER IN
THE NECKS SO THIS IS
THE HANDLE AREA OF YOUR STRIPS.

TO BETTER MAINTAIN EVEN STRIPS, THEY
SHOULD BE MATCHED ON EACH BOW AS I
INDICATED IN MY SKETCH. 1 GOES WITH
1, 2 GOES WITH 2, ETC....

KEEP YOUR HIDE AND STRIPS DRY UNTIL USED.

132

13)

HEAD OF DEER
END, BOW HANDLE

TAIL END,
TIPS

THIS IS THE POINT WHERE YOU JUMP IN IF
YOU BOUGHT YOUR STRIPS. MOST OF THE TIME
THEY WILL STILL REQUIRE SCRAPING WITH A
SHARP KNIFE TO REMOVE FAT. FAT PREVENTS
A GOOD BOND. I GLUE MY STRIPS FLESH
SIDE DOWN, HAIR SIDE UP. IT REALLY
DOESN'T MATTER BUT THE HAIR SIDE IS
USUALLY MORE SMOOTH.

SCRAPE CAREFULLY AVOIDING CUTTING INTO THE
HIDE FOLLOWED BY SANDING WITH A
BLOCK AND 80 GRIT. I SOMETIMES GO AS
FAR AS SANDING THE HANDLE ENDS INTO
TAPERS TO MAKE THE JOINT LESS ABRUPT.

(a)

(b)

SANDED

WITH STRIPS ON THE THINNER SIDE THIS STEP
IS NOT NECESSARY.

133

14) TRIMMING THE HIDE STRIPS: MANY PEOPLE DON'T TAKE THIS STEP, BUT MY GOAL IS TO APPLY MY STRIPS AS NEATLY AS POSSIBLE. I TRIM THE STRIPS TO THE SHAPE OF THE BOW BEFORE GLUING TO THE BACK.

(a) PLACE THE STRIPS ON A FLAT SURFACE, FLESH SIDE UP, OVERLAPPING THE (NECK END) STRIPS MORE THAN AN INCH.

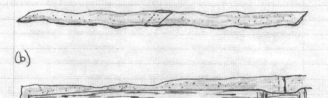

(b)

PLACE THE BOW OVER THE STRIPS BACK-SIDE-DOWN AND TRACE THE BOW SHAPE ONTO THE RAWHIDE. THIS IS IMPORTANT: CUT THE HIDE OUTSIDE OF THE LINES TO ALLOW THE HIDE TO BEND OVER AND DOWN THE SIDES OF THE BOW. THIS HELPS THE HIDE GRIP THE BOW WHILE THE GLUE SETS UP.

$\frac{1}{8}$" INCH MARGIN

PENCIL LINE - DRAWN DARKER FOR CLARITY

134

15) <u>SOAKING THE STRIPS</u>: I BEGIN MY STRIP
SOAKING BY ADDING DEGREASER TO THE WATER.
MY CHOICE IS A CITRUS BASED PRODUCT THAT
IS NON TOXIC, WORKS WELL, AND SMELLS
NICE. DISH SOAP ALSO WORKS WELL. I SOAK
MY STRIPS FOR AN HOUR OR SO ... UNTIL THEY
SOFTEN. FOLLOWING THIS BATH I SCRUB THEM
WITH A BRUSH (CLEAN) AND WASH THEM IN
SEVERAL CHANGES OF CLEAN WATER. FOLLOW
THIS BY REMOVING EXCESS WATER AND PULLING
THEM THROUGH A CLEAN, DRY TOWEL. ROLL
THEM TIGHTLY AND PLACE THEM IN A ZIP
LOCK BAG.

16) <u>PREPARING THE BACK OF THE BOW</u>:
    (a) STAVE BOW / SINGLE GROWTH RING —
    THE BACKS OF SINGLE GROWTH RING BOWS
    ARE NOT AS POROUS AS BIAS RING
    BOARD BOWS SO MORE CARE MUST BE
    TAKEN: i) SCRATCH THE BACK FROM END
    TO END WITH A FINE TOOTHED SAW
    BLADE OR 36 GRIT. ii) WASH THE BACK
    WITH SOAP AND WATER OR WITH A
    SOLVENT. I GO AS FAR AS TO DEGREASE
    BOWS THAT I SHAPED WITH HEAT AND
    GREASE WITH A LYE SOLUTION. THIS IS
    A TECHICAL AND RISKY TECHNIQUE, AND
    BEYOND THE SCOPE OF THIS NOTEBOOK.

                                    135

(6) RED OAK BOARD BOW — RED OAK IS A
SPECIES OF TREE. RED OAK IS ALSO A
GROUP. BELIEVE IT OR NOT, THAT RED
OAK BOARD, MAY NOT BE NORTHERN RED
OAK, BUT ANY OTHER SPECIES WITHIN THE
RED OAK GROUP.,,. BLACK OAK, PIN OAK,
SOUTHERN RED OAK, LAUREL OAK, ETC.

ALTHOUGH THERE MAY BE DIFFERENCES IN
HARDNESS TO SOME MINOR DEGREE, WHAT
THEY ALL HAVE IN COMMON IS THEIR
WIDE OPEN PORES. UNLIKE THE WHITE
OAKS WHOSE PORES ARE CLOGGED WITH
TYLOSES, THE REDS ARE WIDE OPEN
AND READY TO ACCEPT GLUE. DEGREASING
ISN'T A STEP I USUALLY TAKE WHEN
BACKING BOARD BOWS. IF YOU WISH, GO
AHEAD AND WASH THE BACKS WITH SOAP.
IF YOU DON'T, THERE'S NO NEED TO LOSE
SLEEP.

MY PREPARATION OF A RED OAK'S BACK
IS LIMITED TO A FEW END TO END
STROKES WITH 80 GRIT.

17) PREPARING MY WORK STATION: MY
WORK STATION INCLUDE EVERYTHING NEEDED

136

TO GET THE JOB DONE BUT IT CENTERS
AROUND A MEANS OF HOLDING MY WORK
PIECE. YOU MAY USE A PADDED VICE,
TWO CHAIRS, TWO STACKS OF BOOKS....
THERE ARE INDEED MAY WAYS THAT WILL
WORK. I HAPPEN TO USE A FIXTURE THAT
I BUILT FOR SINEW BACKING BOWS.

My JIG

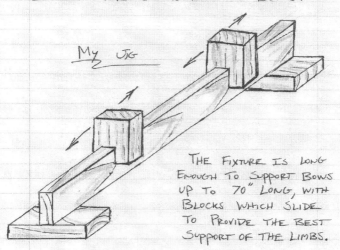

THE FIXTURE IS LONG
ENOUGH TO SUPPORT BOWS
UP TO 70" LONG, WITH
BLOCKS WHICH SLIDE
TO PROVIDE THE BEST
SUPPORT OF THE LIMBS.

IF NEEDED, THE BOW CAN BE
TIED TO THE FIXTURE WITH UNWAXED
DENTAL FLOSS WHICH IS EASILY PULLED
OUT FROM UNDER THE BACKING.

137

OTHER ESSENTIAL ITEMS IN MY WORK STATION ARE:

 TITEBOND II - I USE BOTH
TITEBOND II AND HIDE GLUE.
T.B. II IS VERY CONVENIENT
ALONG WITH WORKING VERY
WELL, SO GO AHEAD AND
SAVE THE HIDE GLUE AND
DOUBLE BOILER FOR SINEW
BACKING.

A COFFEE MUG
FILLED WITH SOAPY
WATER. A FEW
DROPS OF DAWN WILL
WORK.

NEWSPAPER,

PAPER TOWELS,
TWO ROLLS OF GAUZE,
A BOW, RAWHIDE,
AND NETFLIX ......
HAWAII FIVE-O

138

18) GLUING HIDE TO BOW :

(a) MY THEORY — LESS CAN BE MORE. IT
DOESN'T TAKE FLOWING RIVERS OF GLUE TO
BOND RAWHIDE TO A BOW. IT TAKES A
SIZING LAYER ON THE BOW, A VERY THIN
BUT EVEN LAYER ON THE WOOD AFTER SIZING,
A VERY THIN LAYER ON THE HIDE, AND
EVEN PRESSURE. WRAPPING ISN'T 100%
NECESSARY WITH USING A MINIMUM OF GLUE.
IT IS REALLY JUST INSURANCE.

(b) PLAYING ZONES!

ZONE DIAGRAM

I BREAK A BOW INTO ZONES WHEN I
RAWHIDE BACK. I ALWAYS WORK FROM
RIGHT TO LEFT (PERSONAL PREFERENCE) BUT
THE GENERAL THEME SHOULD FOLLOW MY
PROCEDURE.

i) BEGINNING IN AREA 3, RUB SOAPY WATER
ONTO THE LIMB AND ALONG THE EDGES,
FOLLOWED BY A THIN LAYER OF GLUE,
PROVIDING FULL, EVEN COVERAGE. CONTINUE
UNTIL THE ENTIRE LIMB IS SIZED.
MAKE SURE THE EDGES ALONG WITH

139

A LINE ALONG THE UPPER HALF OF THE SIDES ARE SIZED, ALONG WITH THE ENDS OF THE TIPS...

ii) REMOVE ONE OF THE ROLLED HIDE STRIPS FROM THE ZIP LOCK BAG AND LAY IT FLESH SIDE DOWN ON THE LIMB TO THE RIGHT, COVERING AREAS 1, 2, AND 3, THE HANDLE END SHOULD BEGIN AT THE DASHED LINE IN THE ZONE DIAGRAM, LEFT OF CENTER.

iii) STRETCH THE HIDE GENTLY TOWARD THE TIP. HOLDING IT IN PLACE AT THE HANDLE GIVE IT PRESSURE AS YOU SWEEP ALONG IT'S LENGTH TOWARD THE RIGHT WITH YOUR RIGHT HAND, CENTERING AND LENGTHENING.

iv) EXPOSE THE WOOD UNDER AREA 1 BY RAISING THE HIDE AND FLIPPING IT OVER ONTO AREA 2. RUB A VERY THIN EVEN LAYER OF GLUE OVER THE WOOD, AND VERY CAREFULLY ON THE HIDE YOU FLIPPED OVER, AND RETURN IT TO THE BACK OF THE BOW. WITH GENTLE PRESSURE, STRETCH IT BACK TO THE DASHED LINE.

140

u) Taking hold of the rawhide at the tip, fold it over onto the other limb, ending the fold where you left off, between area 1 and 2 (the end of your last line of glue should be obvious). Smear an even, thin layer of glue over area 2, wood and hide, and roll the hide back over area 2. Press, stretch, center.

ui) Repeat with area 3, then fold the hide over the tip and trim so it does not go over the belly of the tip.

* NOTE: If you were wondering why you didn't size areas 4, 5, and 6, it was because you do not want glue to get on the back of the hide when it was folded over any of these sections.

uii) To back the other limb, repeat these steps on the other side. Be sure to size the area of rawhide at the handle where the 2ND hide overlaps

141

19) WRAPPING THE HIDE : ALTHOUGH IT IS VERY POSSIBLE TO BACK A RAWHIDE BOW WITHOUT WRAPPING... THE EDGES DRY FIRST, BONDING BEFORE THE CENTER DRIES AND BEGINS TO SHRINK FULLY ..., I DO WRAP THE BOW WITH GAUZE FOR ADDED INSURANCE.

(a) CONTINUE TO PRESS, CENTER, STRETCH (GENTLY) UNTIL THE EDGES GET STICKY. UNLESS YOU WRAP THE BOW WITH EVEN PRESSURE, YOU RISK SLIPPING THE HIDE SIDEWAYS, EXPOSING AREAS OF THE BACK. WAITING A LITTLE BIT FOR THE EDGES TO GET TACKY, ALONG WITH BEING CAREFUL WHILE WRAPPING CAN KEEP THE HIDE RUNNING STRAIGHT DOWN THE BOW.

(b) BEGINNING AT THE HANDLE WRAP THE GAUZE OVER ITSELF TO KEEP IT IN PLACE AND WITH EVEN PRESSURE, MUMMIFY YOUR BOW. AS YOU WRAP YOUR WAY TOWARD THE TIP, BE CAREFUL TO WATCH YOUR HIDE, KEEPING IT CENTERED AND STRETCHING IT AWAY FROM THE LEADING EDGE OF YOUR WRAP.
* DON'T TRY TO WRAP SUPER TIGHTLY — THIS IS A GOOD WAY TO FORCE THE HIDE SIDEWAYS — USE EVEN PRESSURE.

142

WITH A NEW ROLL OF GAUZE THERE WILL
BE A LOT LEFT OVER WHEN YOU REACH
THE END. DO LET THE GAUZE WRAP
OVER THE TIP SO IT PUSHES THE HIDE
OVER THE TIP. SIMPLY BACK TRACK
TOWARD THE HANDLE, AND SLIP THE
REMAINING PORTION OF GAUZE UNDER THE
PREVIOUS WRAP TO SECURE IT IN PLACE

(C) REPEAT ON THE OTHER LIMB.

(d) I DIDN'T ASK YOU TO WRAP IT "GORILLA
TIGHT" SIMPLY TO AVOID RUINING THE
ALIGNMENT OF THE HIDE. TIGHT WRAPPING
IS GOOD, SO AFTER 6 HOURS OR SO,
UNWRAP THE BOW AND RE-WRAP TIGHTER,
WITH THE GLUE HAVING SET UP, THERE
IS LESS RISK, SO GO AHEAD AND PUT
HEAVIER PRESSURE ON THE GAUZE. THIS
IS AN OPTIONAL STEP. IT IS NOT 100%
NECESSARY. IN ANY CASE, ALLOW THE
BOW TO DRY 24 HOURS AS A MUMMY BOW.

20) FINISHING THE BACKING: YOU MAY
UNWRAP THE BOW AND ALLOW IT TO DRY
IN THE OPEN AIR AFTER 24 HOURS. WAIT
TWO DAYS THOUGH BEFORE YOU TRIM THE
HIDE WITH A SANDING BLOCK.

143

(a) ALWAYS WORK WITH YOUR SANDING BLOCKS
IN A DIRECTION THAT PUSHES THE
RAWHIDE TOWARDS THE BOW'S BACK
OR IN LINE WITH THE EDGE OF THE
LIMBS.

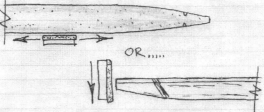

OR.....

I TEND TO BE A LITTLE AMBITIOUS, USING
80 GRIT. 100 GRIT MAY BE A BETTER
CHOICE AS A STARTER GRIT.

(b)

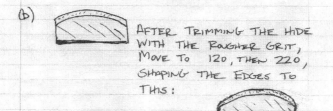

AFTER TRIMMING THE HIDE
WITH THE ROUGHER GRIT,
MOVE TO 120, THEN 220,
SHAPING THE EDGES TO
THIS:

144

(C) TO CLEAN UP THE STRING GROOVES USE THE 3/16" ROUND RASP FOLLOWED WITH A WRAP OF 120 AROUND THE SMALLER END OF THE RASP.

* NOTE: I HAVE SHOWN TRIMMING THE HIDE FLUSH WITH THE EDGES OF THE LIMBS. I DO THIS BECAUSE I EITHER USE HELMSMAN SPAR URETHANE OR MINWAX ULTIMATE FLOOR FINISH TO SEAL AND PROTECT THE BACKING AND THE WOOD.

BOTH URETHANE AND POLYURETHANE ACT AS A GLUE AND SEAL EDGES VERY WELL. IF YOU ARE GOING WITH A MORE PRIMITIVE FINISH, I WOULD SUGGEST NOT TRIMMING THE EDGES — LEAVE THEM INTACT AND OVERLAPPING THE EDGES OF THE LIMBS.

145

21) FINISHING THE BOW: IN A MODERATE CLIMATE (THERE CAN BE GREATER OR LESS DRY TIMES) LIKE MY HOME STATE OF MICHIGAN, I WAIT A WEEK FOR THE BACKING AND WOOD TO COMPLETELY DRY BEFORE I FINISH TILLER. THAT MAY SEEM LIKE A LONG TIME, BUT JUST WAIT UNTIL YOU SINEW BACK AND MEASURE TIME IN MONTHS!!

CAREFULLY FINE TILLER THE BOW USING THE METHODS ALREADY COVERED AND BE SURE TO REFINE YOUR TIPS AND HANDLE. SANDING THE RAWHIDE SURFACE WITH 320 GRIT IS UP TO YOU. I DON'T ALWAYS SAND BECAUSE A ROUGHER SURFACE REFLECTS LIGHT LESS THAN A SMOOTH SURFACE. I USE A COMBINATION OF DYES AND ACRYLIC PAINTS IF I DECORATE THE BOW WHICH IS COMPATABLE WITH POLYURETHANES AND URETHANES. I NEED TO MENTION THAT MANY DYES CAN RUN WHEN PAINTED WITH A FINISHING COAT SO BE CAREFUL.

TWO COATS OF HELMSMAN SPAR, OR MINWAX ULTIMATE FLOOR FINISH IS A GOOD WORKING LAYER.

BRACE BETWEEN 6 AND 7 INCHES. FINI

146

Chapter 6

Project Bow #3
"The Gull Wing"

An Adventure In
Sinew Backing &
Green Wood Shaping

As excited as I may be to describe my journey into the realm of the "Bows of Wood", this particular bow, the sinew backed gull wing holds as much interest for me as any bow could. This short, powerful weapon's evolution followed the rise of the horse culture on America's Great Plains.

Before the appearance of the "sacred dogs", the people were on foot. They most likely were armed with longer bows, skirting the vast open expanses of grass. Once they were able to mount these large, fast creatures, their culture, as well as their bows evolved. They became highly mobile warriors and hunters, moving deeply into these once foreboding areas, following the bison as equals.

These are simple bows. They are physically small, easy to tiller owning to their size along with the deflexed limbs, and in the greater scheme of things, easy to sinew back..... Because they are small. As the people who used these bows were warriors, not soldiers, they

147

Decorated their bows in individual ways:
Dyed, Painted, Adorned with Plaited
Porcupine Quills..... Almost Becoming Living
Creatures In Their own Way.

These are Low Brace, short, Unanchored
Draw Bows. They Perform their Duties on
Their Terms. That Is One of The Things
Which I Respect About Them: Unlike A
Silky Smooth, Full Draw Longbow, A Bow
Such as a Gullwing Demands That You Do
Things Their Way. Once You Understand That
You Will Find Out How Well These "Little
Monsters" Do Their Job. With Practice
They Are Very Capable Hunting Weapon
Fully Able To Bring Down A Bison As
Well as a Squirrel.

The Original Bows Ranged Between
40 to 50 Inches In Length ~ Some
Shorter Some Longer. The Real
Beauty Being That The Bow, Arrows, Along
With Other Items Such As Awls And Fire
Making Tools Were All Carried In One
Neat Package Known As A Plains Quiver
And Bow Case. This Mobile And Compact
Package Could Be Slung Over The
Rider's Back, Combining Style With
Function.

148

It would be wrong on my part to give you the impression that this is the one and only form of bow used on horse back. One could say that the typical horse bow is shorter than most bows, but even that wouldn't be very accurate. I would feel more comfortable to say that they were of a minimul length and stop there. Horse bows were backed, unbacked as in the case of the Comanche, sometimes horn and sinew in the case of the Sheep Eaters, and randomly made with horn bellies.... Some were gull wings, some cupid bow shaped, some straight limbed, tips deflexed, some with deflexed handled and big recurves.... There was no one type of horse bow.... Warriors not soldiers.

I often wonder how this form came into being:

A) Did it begin with a simple D bow gained a lot of string follow?

149

"UNDERSTANDING
SOMETHING SHOULD ALSO
INCLUDE HOW THAT SOME-
THING CAME TO BE...."

B).... SO THEY FIXED THE
SITUATION BY SIMPLY
SETTING THE HANDLE
BACK?

C)....AND THEN DISCOVERING
THAT THIS SHAPE
HOLDS OTHER ADVANTAGES
BEYOND CURING STRING
FOLLOW?

I HAVE READ THAT ONE ADVANTAGE OF
BENDING BOWS IN THIS WAY IS IN HOW IT
REDUCES THE LENGTH WITHOUT REDUCING THE
ACTUAL LENGTH OF THE BOW. IT DOES TO
SOME EXTENT, BUT IN REAL TERMS THE
OTHER ADVANTAGES THIS DESIGN HOLDS FAR OVER
SHADOW SHORTENING A BOW BY MAYBE AN INCH.

150

I BELIEVE THAT THERE ARE THREE THINGS
THAT GO ON WHEN A BOW IS SHAPED INTO A
GULL WING:

(a) WHEN THE LIMBS ARE DEFLEXED, AN AMOUNT
OF "STRING FOLLOW" IS INDUCED WHICH MAY
PRE-COMPRESS THE FIBERS IN THE BELLY AND
PRE-STRETCH THE FIBERS IN THE BACK TO
A POINT OF EQUALIBRIUM. IN EFFECT, YOU
ARE BENDING THE LIMBS, HITTING "A WALL",
ALLOWING THE LIMBS TO WORK WITHOUT GAINING
MORE FOLLOW UNLESS PUSHED BEYOND IT'S
LIMITS. THEN BY REFLEXING THE HANDLE,
THE BOW IS THEN "STRING FOLLOW PROOF."

(b) "LIFT WITH YOUR LEGS, NOT YOUR BACK". WHAT
I HAVE WITNESSED IN SHORT BOWS THAT ARE
DEFLEXED, GULL WINGS INCLUDED, IS THAT
HAVING THAT BACKWARDS CURVE CHANGES THE
GEOMETRY OF THE BEND, ALLOWING THEM
TO BEND FARTHER WITH MORE EASE.

(c) FINALLY, DEFLEXING THE LIMBS THROUGHOUT
SUCH A LARGE PERCENTAGE OF THEIR LENGTH
MAKES TILLERING EASIER. SIMPLY PUT, TILLERING
A GULL WING BOW IS SO MUCH LESS
TEMPERAMENTAL THAN TILLERING A LONGER
STRAIGHT LIMBED BOW, AND FAR, FAR EASIER
THAN A RECURVED AND RELEXED PADDLE BOW
OF THE SAME LENGTH.

1) WORKING THE WOOD: THESE BOWS COULD EASILY BE MADE FROM LARGE STAVES, AS WE AS WORKED DOWN TO THE HEARTWOOD IN OSAGE AS WELL AS FROM A BOARD. THERE IS A GREAT LATITUDE AFFORDED TO US IN THE DESIGN OF A GULL WING. IN MY MIND, A PERFECT PROJECT BOW, YOUR FIRST THREE BEND BOW SHOULD BE SIMPLE, FOLLOWING A SPECIFIC LAKOTA BOW THAT I SAW IN A MUSEUM. THIS ARTIFACT WAS MADE FROM A SMALL ENOUGH STAVE TO SHOW THE PITH ON THE BELLY. THE SINEW BACKING WAS ROUGH, THERE WERE TOOL MARKS ON THE BELLY, AND IT HAD A SUBTLE BEND.

(a) SEARCH OUT A STRAIGHT SECTION OF HARDWOOD 2 TO 3 INCHES IN DIAMETER, ABOUT 50 INCHES LONG.

(b) CONSIDER THIS AS SIMPLE AS A "D" BOW: SPLIT OR SHAVE THE SAPLING FLAT ON THE BELLY AND THEN WORK IT INTO A STRAIGHT SHAPE, 1½" WIDE IN THE CENTER, TAPERING TO 1" AT THE TIP. SHAPE THE HANDLE AND TIPS AS SHOWN IN THE DIAGRAM.

①

SPLITTING THE ROUND

②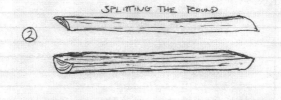

ROUGHING THE FACE

③
$1\frac{1}{2}''$ $1''$

ROUGHED OUT BOW

 ④

⑤ HANDLE & TIPS

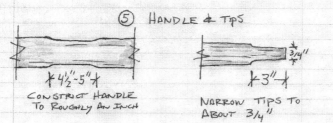

$4\frac{1}{2}''-5''$ $3''$ $3/4''$

CONSTRICT HANDLE
TO ROUGHLY AN INCH

NARROW TIPS TO
ABOUT 3/4''

WITH THIS BOW I AM GIVING YOU NUMBERS
IN TERMS OF "ABOUT" OR "AROUND" EXACTLY
BECAUSE "FOLLOWING YOUR EYE" NEEDS TO BE
AS IMPORTANT AS FOLLOWING STRICT DIMENSIONS.
ALWAYS WORK ON DEVELOPING A SENSE OF
RATIO AND PROPORTION.

2) THINNING THE STAVE: * I HAVE ALSO MADE
GULL WINGS WHICH AREN'T BACKED. THE KEY
TO THIS IS LEAVING ENOUGH WOOD IN THE
HANDLE TO KEEP THE SET BACK FROM PULLING
OUT. THIS IS A DIFFERENCE BETWEEN A GULL
WING AND A D BOW: A RELATIVELY THICKER
SECTION THROUGH THE CENTER.

(a) THINNING BY EYE — IF YOU ARE GOING "OLD
SCHOOL" AND YOUR WORKING BY EYES WITHOUT
SCRIBING LINES FOR THICKNESS, FLOOR TILLERING
IS YOUR GUIDE. GENTLY BEND AND THIN
UNTIL YOU ACHIEVE AN EVEN BEND IN EACH
LIMB STARTING FROM SEVERAL INCHES BEYOND
THE HANDLE FADES, THROUGH THE LIMBS,
ENDING JUST BEFORE THE TIP FADES.
DO NOT ALLOW ANY BENDING THROUGH THE
HANDLE, AND DO LEAVE A SUBTLE "BUMP" IN
THICKESS IN THE HANDLE.

HANDLE CENTER

154

(b) <u>SCRIBING THICKNESS</u> — YOUR LINES WILL REDUCE THE THICKNESS IN THREE STEPS: 3/4", 1/2", AND 3/8". AT THIS POINT, PRIOR TO SHAPING THE BENDS, IT IS NOT 100% NECESSARY FOR ONE STEP TO GRADE SMOOTHLY INTO THE NEXT STEP. IT IS ACTUALLY EASIER TO SMOOTH THE STEPS WITH A SANDING BLOCK AFTER YOUR STAVE HAS DRIED. AS FAR AS THE GREEN STAVE IS CONCERNED, IT JUST NEEDS TO BE CLOSE TO ALLOW THE BOW TO BEND SMOOTHLY ON THE BENDING FORM.

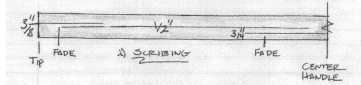

i) SCRIBING

3/8" TIP — FADE — 1/2" — 3/4" — FADE — CENTER HANDLE

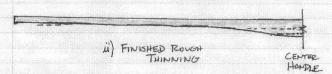

ii) FINISHED ROUGH THINNING

CENTER HANDLE

* SCRIBING LINES GIVES YOU A REFERENCE MORE SO THAN HARD AND FAST LINES TO WORK DOWN TO — THERE IS NO ABSOLUTE WAY TO AVOID HAVING TO DEVELOP A TRAINED EYE.

155

3) GREEN WUD BENDING - IT WOULD BE A MISTAKE
ON MY PART TO CONVEY THE IDEA THAT ONE
CAN BEND GREEN WOOD TO THE EXTENT OF
CAUSING DAMAGE TO THE CELLS OF THE WOOD,
BUT WHEN IT DRYS THE DAMAGE WILL BE
NULLIFIED. ALWAYS BE ON GUARD WHEN FORCING
WOOD INTO A BEND. CONVINCE THE WOOD TO BEND,
HELP THE WOOD TO BEND .... APPROACH IT IN
A WAY OF REQUESTING MORE SO THAN BARKING
ORDERS AT YOUR STAVE.

YOU SHALL BE PUTTING A BACKWARDS BEND INTO
YOUR HANDLE AND THE BEST WAY TO APPROACH
THAT GENTLY YET FIRMLY. IT DOESN'T NEED
TO BE AN INSTANT PROCESS - LASH YOUR HANDLE
TO A BOARD OR SECTION OF FENCE RAIL AND
BLOCK THE LIMBS UP. I USE ROUNDS THAT
WERE TRIMMED FROM THE ENDS OF THE STAVE.
FEEL HOW FAR YOU CAN BEND THE LIMBS
EASILY AND REACH THAT POINT - AND STOP.
IF YOU WAIT, AND THEN PUSH THE ROUNDS
CLOSER TO THE HANDLE, HOW MUCH PRESSURE
DOES IT TAKE?

WAYS TO INCREASE THE BEND WITHOUT CAUSING
DAMAGE TO THE HANDLE INCLUDE POURING
BOILING WATER ON THE HANDLE, APPLYING HEAT
WITH A HEAT GUN OR HOLDING THE HANDLE
OVER COALS, OR EVEN STEAMING THE HANDLE,

156

BENDING IT BACKWARDS OVER YOUR KNEE, THEN
LASHING IT ONTO YOUR BOARD. KEEP IN MIND
THAT THE BEND THROUGH THE HANDLE DOES
NOT NEED TO BE SEVERE. APACHE BOWS
MAY HAVE HAD EXTREME SET BACK, BUT
THE MAJORITY OF GULL WINGS WERE SUBTLE.

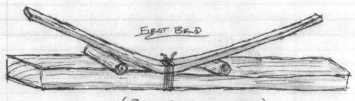

FIRST BEND

(BEND IS EXAGGERATED)

ONCE THE HANDLE IS SET BACK, THE HARD
PART IS OVER. JUST IN CASE THERE WAS
A MINOR SPLIT IN THE BELLY, GLUE AND
SINEW WRAPPING CAN SECURE IT, PROVIDED
THAT IT WAS MINOR. THE NEXT STEP
IS TO DEFLEX THE LIMBS. BECAUSE THE
HANDLE IS THICKER THAN THE LIMBS, AND
THAT BEND IS MORE SEVERE, COUNT ON
SOME LOSS OF BEND, SO DO NOT LET THE
TIPS TOUCH THE BOARD WHEN YOU LASH
THEM DOWN. LET THEM FLOAT ABOUT AN
INCH ABOVE THE BOARD. SIGHT DOWN THE
BOW TO MAKE SURE YOU HAVE A STRAIGHT STAVE.

157

DEFLEXING THE
LIMBS —

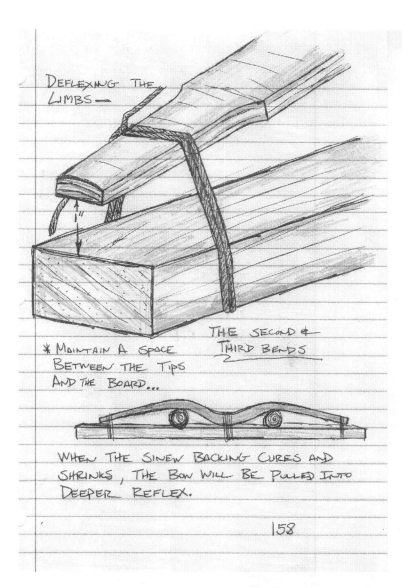

THE SECOND &
THIRD BENDS

* MAINTAIN A SPACE
BETWEEN THE TIPS
AND THE BOARD...

WHEN THE SINEW BACKING CURES AND
SHRINKS, THE BOW WILL BE PULLED INTO
DEEPER REFLEX.

158

4) LETTING THE BOW CURE: THIS IS A DIFFERENT SITUATION THAN WORKING A GREEN WOOD SELF BOW BECAUSE THE OVERALL DRYING OF THE BOW WILL CONTINUE ALONG WITH THE CURING OF THE SINEW. WHAT WE NEED TO DO IS SIMPLY ALLOW THE BOW TO DRY ENOUGH TO RETAIN IT'S SHAPE ALONG WITH BEING DRY ENOUGH TO BACK. SIMPLE ... GIVEN THOSE NEEDS WE CAN MOST LIKELY BE READY TO BOND SINEW TO WOOD IN ONLY A MATTER OF WEEKS.

a) I PREFER TO LET THE FIRST PHASE OF DRYING PROCEED SLOWLY. THIS IS THE STAGE WHERE THE BOW CONTAINS THE GREATEST AMOUNT OF MOISTURE SO IT WILL SPEND SEVERAL DAYS IN THE DARK, OUT OF THE WIND. IT MAY HELP TO MAINTAIN A HIGHER MOISTURE CONTENT IN THE BEGINNING TO ALLOW THE CURVES SET INTO THE WOOD A BIT BETTER. KEEP IN MIND THAT THE BOW IS STILL FIGHTING THOSE BINDINGS SO IF YOU WISH TO POUR BOILING HOT WATER OVER IT AT SET INTERVALS, FEEL FREE TO DO SO. IT CAN ONLY HELP.

159

(b) Exposure to wind and sunlight should begin after several days of slow drying. This time is added to the total time. If you were pouring hot water over the bends — without the water treatment, two days in a still place after lashing to the board... with the hot water treatment, two days drying in a still place after that last hot bath.

Drying times vary so much, depending upon your local weather. In Michigan during the spring and fall, I would give it three weeks outside in the wind and sun. In the summer, possibly two weeks. In the dry air of winter, in the house with a fan blowing air over it, perhaps two weeks.

These times are vague but unless you have a moisture meter, it is all guess work. One key is to untie it after a period of time and judge the bend retention, how the belly reacts to sanding, and

160

HOW LIGHT THE BOW FEELS. AGAIN, IT WILL HAVE SEVERAL MONTHS TO DRY AFTER BEING SINEW BACKED SO IT DOESN'T NEED TO BE AT 9% OR EVEN TILLERED AT THIS POINT.

AS FAR AS WE ARE CONCERNED AT THIS POINT, WE ARE DONE WITH WOOD WORKING, EXCEPT FOR PREPARING THE BACK FOR THE APPLICATION OF SINEW.

5) SINEW BACKING: WORKING WITH SINEW DOES NOT NEED TO BE INTIMIDATING. TO MAKE A GOOD WORKING LAYER, IT DOESN'T NEED TO BE SMOOTH OR EVEN. IT CAN HAVE GAPS, LUMPS, WAVES, AND STILL WORK WELL. THERE ARE ACTUALLY THREE SCHOOLS OF THOUGHT: A SMOOTH, EVEN, FLAWLESS BACKING IS A BEAUTIFUL THING. THE SECOND THOUGHT IS THAT A ROUGH, TEXTURED, UNEVEN LAYER IS A BEAUTIFUL THING BECAUSE IT LOOKS LIKE A LIVING CREATURE. THE THIRD SCHOOL OF THOUGHT IS THAT IT DOESN'T MATTER WHAT IT LOOKS LIKE BECAUSE IT WORKS WELL EITHER WAY. THE LESSON HERE THAT REALLY MATTERS IS THAT LOOK NICE IN ANY FORM AND

THAT IT WORKS WHETHER IT'S SMOOTH OR
ROUGH. AS MY FRIEND JESSIE SAYS, "IT
DOESN'T HAVE TO BE PRETTY TO WORK."

(9) PREPARING THE GLUE: NO SIR, DO NOT USE
TITEBOND OR LIQUID HIDE GLUE. CONSIDERING HOW
PREPARING THE SINEW TAKES THE BIGGEST
CHUNK OF TIME, WHY BOTHER TO SHAVE A
FEW MINUTES OFF OF THE TOTAL TIME WHEN
ACTUAL HOT HIDE GLUE GIVES THE BEST RESULTS.
HEAT IS YOUR FRIEND AND THAT FRIEND AWAITS
YOU IN A BIG COFFEE MUG FLOATING IN A PAN
OF WATER SITTING ON A HUMBLE HOT PLATE.

POWDERED HIDE GLUE AS WELL AS DRIED TENDONS
CAN BE PURCHASED FROM A PRIMITIVE ARCHERY
SUPPLY COMPANY. IN ITS POWDERED FORM,
IT WILL LAST FOR YEARS IN YOUR FREEZER SO
DO NOT WORRY ABOUT BUYING TOO MUCH. BUY
HALF A POUND AND YOU WILL BE SET TO MAKE
MORE THAN A FEW BOWS.

HOW YOU MIX THE GLUE ISN'T ALL THAT CRITICAL.
FILLING THE CUP HALF WAY WITH THE POWDER AND
THEN TOPPING OFF THE CUP WITH COLD WATER WILL

162

WORK NICELY. IT ONLY NEEDS TO BE MIXED
THICKLY ENOUGH SO IT GELS AT ROOM TEMPERATURE.
ALLOW IT TO SIT FOR SEVERAL HOURS BEFORE
HEATING.

GLUE CAN ALSO BE MADE FROM SINEW SCRAPS:
SAVE UP ALL OF THE BITS AND PIECES THAT
BUILD UP WHEN YOU STRIP YOUR TENDONS AND
SQUIRREL THEM AWAY IN A PAPER GROCERY
BAG. WHEN THE BAG IS HALF FULL, PLACE
THE TENDONS INTO A BIG POT OF WATER AND
SIMMER ON LOW HEAT UNTIL THEY BREAK
DOWN. SCREEN OUT THE LITTLE CURLY BITS
AND POUR THE "TENDON SOUP" IN A SHALLOW
PAN LINED WITH A GARBAGE BAG, ALLOW IT
TO DRY, WITH A FAN BLOWING OVER IT,
AND EVENTUALLY YOU WILL BE LEFT WITH AN
AMBER SHEET THAT CAN BE BROKEN APART
AND TURNED BACK INTO GLUE.

(b) PREPARING THE TENDONS: FOR A BOW OF THIS
SIZE, PREPARE 10 BOW READY WHITE TAIL
TENDONS INTO SINEW. I PREFER WHITE TAIL,
BUT YOU CAN CERTAINLY USE ELK TENDONS, OR
OSTRICH, OR BISON, OR BACKSTRAP... JUST DON'T

163

SKIMP ON PRICE AND TRY COW TENDONS. THE WHOLE POINT OF RAISING CATTLE IS TO FATTEN THEM UP AS FAST AS POSSIBLE AND IT SHOWS: COW TENDONS ARE GROSS. GREASY, STINKY SINEW IS NOT FUN TO WORK WITH. STICK WITH DEER AND YOU WILL BE A HAPPY CAMPER.

A PEARL OF WISDOM IS TO STRIP THEM DRY. YOU WILL GIVE YOURSELF SORE FINGERS AND THERE WILL BE A BIT MORE WASTE THEN THE DAMP STRIPPING METHOD. HOWEVER, IF YOU WET STRIP THEM THEY NEED TO STAY WET AND DRY SINEW WILL ABSORB GLUE BETTER. IT IS ALSO FLUFFIER AND EASIER TO WORK WITH.

LEG TENDONS REQUIRE POUNDING. NOT GORILLA STYLE POUNDING, RATHER QUICK MODERATE POUNDING. POUND WITH A SMOOTH FACED HAMMER, A SMOOTH ROUND ROCK, OR CHUCK NORRIS' FISTS. POINT TAKEN. THE SURFACE THAT YOU REST THE TENDONS ON MUST ALSO BE SMOOTH SO FIBERS ARE NOT CUT... SMOOTH CONCRETE, A SMOOTH ROCK... SMOOTH IS THE KEY. QUICK POUNDING LOOSENS FIBERS, LOOSENS THE SHEATH,

164

AND ALLOWS YOU SEPARATE THE TENDONS INTO
THREES PARTS: TWO "y's" AND ONE STRIP.

THE FIRST SECTION THAT FALLS AWAY IS A
SHORT STRIP, THESE SHORTIES ARE RARELY
LONG ENOUGH TO BE OF ANY USE, SO RETURN
IT TO NATURE, OR SAVE IT FOR GLUE.

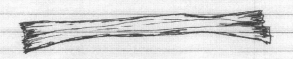

CONTINUE TO POUND AND ROTATE THE TENDON
UNTIL YOU CAN EASILY PULL IT INTO TWO
"y" SHAPED SECTIONS. THE FIRST OF THE
"y's" IS EASY TO PULL INTO FINER FIBERS.
POUND IT ALONG IT'S ENTIRE LENGTH UNTIL
YOU CAN EASILY REMOVE THE SMALL FLAP
AND THE TAGS ON THE ENDS OF THE "y".

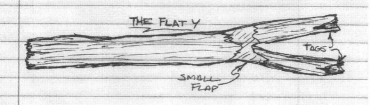

THE FLAT Y

TAGS

SMALL
FLAP

165

THE BIGGER "y" WILL BE MORE OF A CHALLANGE
TO SPLIT INTO SMALLER FIBERS BECAUSE IT
IS BRAIDED. ONE WOULD BELIEVE THAT ONE
COULD PULL IT APART LIKE A WISH BONE,
BUT ONE WOULD BE VERY WRONG. YOU NEED
TO SPLIT I INTO TWO "y's" BEFORE BEING
ABLE TO PULL IT APART LIKE A WISH BONE.

LAY IT ON THE GROUND AND PONDER IT. THAT
IS NOT HOW YOU WILL POUND IT! ROTATE IT
SO THAT IT IS ON THE GROUND WITH ONE
OF THE ARMS OF THE "y" PROUDLY IN THE
AIR.

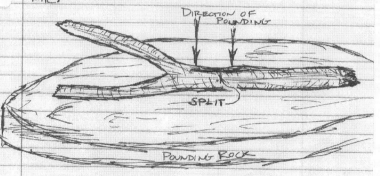

POUND THOROUGHLY AND FLEX UNTIL YOU CAN DEVELOP
A SPLIT AS SHOWN IN THE PICTURE. ONCE YOU

166

CAN DEVELOP A SPLIT AT THE BASE OF THE "Y" - A PRE-Y BASAL CREVICE, AS MANY (NONE REALY) SINEW BACKISTS REFER TO IT, YOU ARE IN BUSINESS... THESE Y'S CAN BE THEN SPLIT INTO TWO EQUAL Y'S EITHER BY HAND OR WITH THE HELP OF A SMOOTH BUTTER KNIFE.

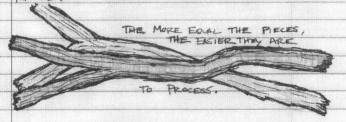

THE MORE EQUAL THE PIECES, THE EASIER THEY ARE TO PROCESS.

FROM THIS POINT, EACH OF YOUR PIECES CAN BE SPLIT LIKE WISHBONES AND REDUCED INTO SMALLER FIBERS.

SMALLER FIBERS... HOW SMALL? DURING THE PROCESS OF REDUCING TENDON INTO USABLE FIBERS, WASTE IS PRODUCED. THE FARTHER YOU PROCEED, THE MORE WASTE YOU DEVELOP. THERE MAY ALSO BE A POINT IN WHICH THE INDIVIDUAL FIBERS MAY BE WEAKENED SO FIGHT THE URGE TO OVERPROCESS.

167

So what does that mean: to overprocess. To what point do you reduce the sinew? The best description I can come up with to convey this in writing is to compare your finished fibers slightly finer than the thickness of a 12 strand B50 bow string. Getting a feeling of how far you can push it comes with experience but this is a safe point to stop. Another important point is to pull the sinew slowly, almost coaxing it apart. Ripping it apart quickly can cause damage.

(c) Prepping the Bow: Preparing a bow's back for sinew backing follows the same game plan as it is done for rawhide backing. Please refer to the section on rawhide backing, pages 135-136 and follow the same procedures.

(d) Preparing the Work Station: The major difference between your sinew backing work station and your rawhide backing work station is the addition of a hot plate and your hide glue..

168

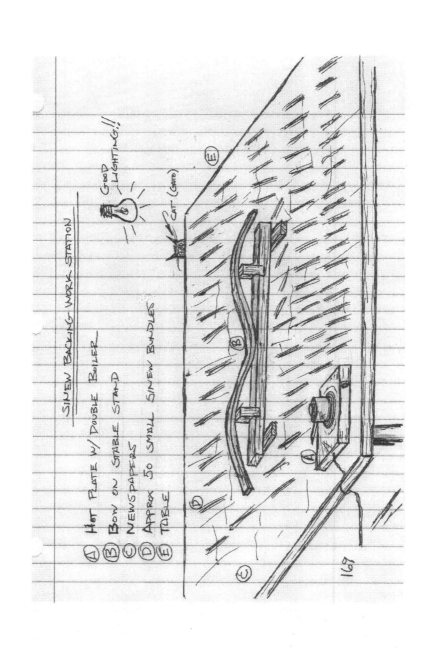

SINEW BACKING WORK STATION

(A) HOT PLATE w/ DOUBLE BOILER
(B) BOW ON STABLE STAND
(C) NEWSPAPERS
(D) APPROX 50 SMALL SINEW BUNDLES
(E) TABLE

GOOD LIGHTING!!

CAT (GATE)

169

(A) HOT PLATE w/ DOUBLE BOILER: HIDE GLUE
AND SINEW GLUE NEEDS TO BE HEATED TO
THE POINT BELOW DISCOMFORT WHEN YOU ARE
DIPPING YOUR BUNDLES. TOO HOT AND THE
SINEW WILL SHRIVEL. TOO COOL AND THE
GLUE WILL GEL ON THE BUNDLES TOO QUICKLY.
HAVING YOUR GLUE POT IN A POT OF WATER ALLOWS
YOU TO BETTER CONTROL THE HEAT MORE
CONSISTENTLY. SMALLER JOBS SUCH AS FLETCHING
ARROWS OR WRAPPING TIPS CAN BE DONE BY
HEATING THE GLUE CAREFULLY IN A MICROWAVE
OR ON A STOVE TOP IN A BIGGER POT OF
WATER — THEN MOVING IT TO YOUR WORK STATION
DOES WORK... BUT FOR BACKING A BOW, CONSIDER
A HOT PLATE NECESSARY.

(B) THE JIG, AS SHOWN ON PAGE 137 WAS
BUILT FOR SINEW BACKING 20 YEARS AGO
AND IS STILL BEING USED. IT'S A GOOD
AND SIMPLE DESIGN THAT AFFORDS SUPPORT
ON BOWS OF DIFFERNT LENGTHS AND SHAPES.
IF I SHOULD BE OF NEED TO REFLEX THE
BOW PRIOR TO BACKING, I SET THE BLOCKS
AT THE TIPS AND TIE THE HANDLE TO THE
JIG TIGHTLY WITH UNWAXED DENTAL FLOSS.

170

C) NEWSPAPERS TO KEEP DRIPPY HIDE GLUE
OFF OF THE TABLE TOP. MORE IMPORTANTLY,
TO KEEP YOUR BEAUTIFUL WIFE HAPPY BECAUSE
THE TABLE ISN'T COVERED WITH DRIPPY HIDE
GLUE — HAPPY WIFE, HAPPY LIFE... LEARN IT
AND LIVE IT.

D) BREAK THAT BIG PILE OF SINEW INTO
SMALL BUNDLES ABOUT THE SIZE OF A PENCIL
IN DIAMETER, EACH SMALL BUNDLE SHOULD
BE COMPOSED OF RANDOM LENGTH FIBERS.
10 DEER LEG TENDONS USUALLY YIELDS APPROX
50 SMALLER BACKING BUNDLES — MY GUESS
IS 47.

E) A TABLE LARGE ENOUGH TO HOLD YOUR ENTIRE
WORK STATION.

GOOD LIGHTING. GOOD LIGHTING, AND GOOD
LIGHTING. I WENT SO FAR AS INSTALLING A
TWO TUBE LIGHT FIXTURE DIRECTLY ABOVE
MY SINEW BACKING STATION.

e) BACKING YOUR BOW: (i) SIZING A SINEW
BACKED BOW IS SIMILAR TO SIZING A RAW

171

HIDE BACKED BOW WITH REALLY ONLY ONE REAL
DIFFERENCE: IT TAKES MORE THAN ONE COATING
OF GLUE. IT TAKES AS MANY COATS AS NEEDED
TO BUILD UP A SHINY SURFACE. IF THE BOW
IS A REALLY HARD WOOD SUCH AS OSAGE OR
BLACK LOCUST, I WILL HEAT THE BOW PRIOR
TO SIZING. OTHER WOOD WILL GENERALLY BE
SIZED AT ROOM TEMPERATURE.

WHEN I APPLY GLUE, I FIRST GIVE THE BOW
A WASH OF WARM WATER WITH A FEW DROPS
OF DISH SOAP ADDED TO HELP THE BOW ABSORB
THE HIDE GLUE. AFTER THIS WASH, I DIP
MY FINGERS FIRST INTO THE HOT WATER IN
THE DOUBLE BOILER, THEN THE GLUE AND
THEN WIPE IT OVER THE BOW. AFTER LETTING
IT DRY, KEEP REPEATING THIS UNTIL THE
BOW'S BACK IS SHINY, AND WILL STICK TO
A DAMPENED FINGER.

(ii) PATTERNS!! PATTERN IS THE WORD OF THE DAY.
A GOOD, UNIFORM SINEW JOB REQUIRES WELL THOUGHT
OUT PATTERNS WHICH ALLOW YOU TO LAY EACH
LAYER CONSISTENTLY, EVEN, AND IN A BRICK-
WORK PATTERN WITH OVERLAPPING JOINTS.

172

HAVING FIBERS OF RANDOM LENGTHS WITHIN EACH OF YOUR SMALLER BUNDLES HELPS TO FORM SMOOTH OVERLAPPING JOINTS WHEN BACKING BOWS WITH MULTIPLE LAYERS. CONSIDER YOUR FIRST HURDLE JUMPED. YOU CAN CERTAINLY LAY A SINGLE LAYER TO KEEP YOUR BACK INTACT, BUT IT TAKES SEVERAL LAYERS TO SHIFT THE NEUTRAL PLANE HELPING THE WOOD IN COMPRESSION ALONG WITH GIVING YOUR BOW THE BENEFIT OF HAVING A WORKING LAYER OF SINEW. A PERCENTAGE I HAVE HEARD ON THE STREETS IS THAT THE BEST THICKNESS IS A SINEW LAYER THAT IS 25% OF THE BOW'S THICKNESS. UP UNTIL THAT POINT, SINEW WILL BEGIN TO WORK SO DON'T FEEL THAT THAT THICKNESS NEEDS TO BE REACHED — EVEN 12½% WILL BE EFFECTIVE.

THERE ARE MANY VARIATIONS OF PATTERNING THAT YOU MAY USE, BUT I WILL SUGGEST A SERIES THAT WILL BE SIMPLE, EASY TO TRACK, AND WILL BUILD UP THE SINEW EFFECTIVELY.

(iii) THE FIRST LAYER WILL COVER THE HANDLE, THE FULL WIDTH OF THE BOW. IT'S IMPORTANT TO GIVE THE HANDLE EXTRA SUPPORT TO PREVENT

173

THE SET BACK FROM PULLING OUT.

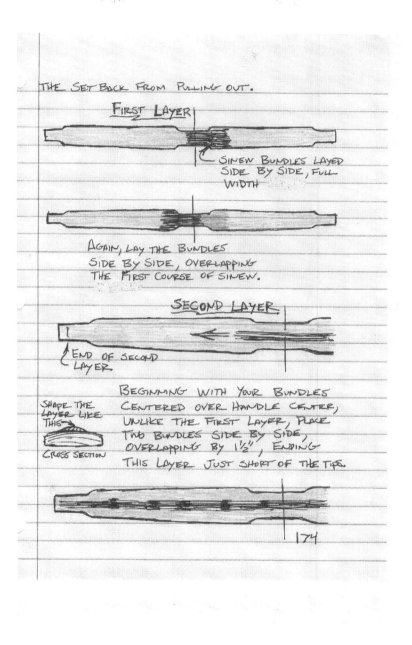

FIRST LAYER

SINEW BUNDLES LAYED
SIDE BY SIDE, FULL
WIDTH

AGAIN, LAY THE BUNDLES
SIDE BY SIDE, OVERLAPPING
THE FIRST COURSE OF SINEW.

SECOND LAYER

END OF SECOND
LAYER.

SHAPE THE
LAYER LIKE
THIS →

CROSS SECTION

BEGINNING WITH YOUR BUNDLES
CENTERED OVER HANDLE CENTER,
UNLIKE THE FIRST LAYER, PLACE
TWO BUNDLES SIDE BY SIDE,
OVERLAPPING BY 1½", ENDING
THIS LAYER JUST SHORT OF THE TIPS.

174

Third Layer

This could be the most controversial of
the layers: Yes, when I build up layers
of sinew I use a more complex brick-
work pattern. Sinew layers blend together
making it difficult to keep track of
where you are leaving off. Being able
to maintain patterns comes with experience.

The following method does work provided
that you practice good overlapping.
* Do go over the edges of the limbs
about an 1/8 of an inch. When you reach
the tips, go over and onto the belly an
inch or two. * To avoid a thick tip after
tillering, thin the tips before sinew backing.

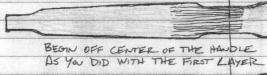

Begin off center of the handle
as you did with the first layer

Maintain a good overlap

175

* WHEN SINEW SHRINKS, IT CAN PULL AWAY
ON INSIDE CURVES :

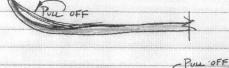

IN THE CASE OF THE RECURVE AND
THE SET BACK IN THE GULL WING, WE
PREVENT THAT BY SUPPORTING THE
SINEW BY WRAPPING THE BOW TIGHTLY
DURING THE PROCESS OF DRYING AND
SHRINKING.

ANOTHER AREA OF CONCERN IS THE
TRANSITION IN WIDTH AT THE HANDLE.
WE ALSO CONTROL WITH WRAPPING, THE
AMOUNT OF PULL OFF. HOWEVER, WE
CAN ALSO CONTROL IT WITH HOW WE
LAY THE BACKING.

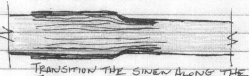

TRANSITION THE SINEW ALONG THE
EDGE ONTO THE BACK OF THE HANDLE.

176

(F) APPLYING SINEW: APPLYING SINEW IS EASY
BUT MESSY; GLUE WILL BUILD UP ON YOUR FINGERS
BUT CAN BE PEELED OFF AND PLOPPED BACK
INTO THE GLUE POT. GLUE WILL DRIP, BUT
IT WILL LAND ON THE NEWSPAPERS. THIS IS
THE DANGEROUS WORLD OF SINEW BACKING...

BEGIN WHEN YOUR GLUE IS HOT, BUT NOT SO HOT
THAT IT MAKES YOUR SINEW SHRIVEL... OOPS,
TEENAGE BOY LEVEL MATURITY CREEPING IN...
TAKE A BUNDLE AND DIP IT IN THE GLUE AND
RELAX YOUR FINGERS SO THE WHOLE LENGTH CAN
SOAK AND COUNT TO 20. SQUEEZE THE
EXCESS GLUE FROM IT, AND SQUEEZE IT
SO THE FIBERS LAY IT A STRAIGHT LINE.
APPLY IT TO THE BOW AND PRESS IT INTO
PLACE,,,, REPEAT THIS APPROXIMATLEY 48
TIMES FOLLOWING MY PATTERNS, WASH
YOUR HANDS AND TAKE AN HOUR BREAK.

(G) WRAPPING YOUR BOW: WRAPPING AT THIS POINT
IS DONE WITH GAUZE. ADDING SINEW WRAPS
TO THE TIPS AND HANDLE MUST BE DONE
AFTER THE BACKING HAS SHRUNK TO ITS
FINISHED THICKNESS.

177

After an hour of drying, the glue
has begun to gel, but it is still soft.
I alway wrap my bows with roll gauze
because that added support aids in making
the backing more even. Authentic Native
backed bows sometimes show the spiral
impressions from bark wrappings so this
technique is nothing new. With a short
bow such as this, one roll will fully
cover the bow, starting at one tip and
moving to the other. I secure my gauze
by going to the end, backing up, and
sliding the gauze under a previous wrapping.

* Do not attempt to wrap tightly. Putting
uneven pressure on the gauze can force the
sinew off center. Wrapping is a skill so
in the beginning, just do your best to
apply an even pressure without bearing
down with great pressure. Allow the
bow to dry overnight at which time you
may rewrap it under greater pressure.
Allow your "Mummy Bow" to dry for two days
before allowing it to dry uncovered for
at least a month and a half under

178

MODERATE CONDITIONS. SINEW CAN TAKE ALMOST
A YEAR TO FULLY CURE. I HAVE FOUND THAT
YOU CAN PUT A BEND INTO A SINEW BACKED
BOW WITHIN SEVERAL MONTHS, BUT I DO
TREAT THEM MORE GENTLY. AFTER SEVERAL
WEEKS YOU MAY HELP THE BOW CURE WITH
WIND AND SUNLIGHT. I SOMETIMES "BAKE"
THEM ON A RACK ABOVE A WOODSTOVE.
YOU DO NEED TO TAKE INTO ACCOUNT, YOUR
LOCAL ENVIRONMENTAL CONDITIONS — DO NOT
RUSH THIS BOW BECAUSE USE BEFORE IT
IS READY WILL STUNT IT'S PERFORMANCE.

ONE INDICATION OF THE CURING PROGRESS
IS THE REFLEX THAT IT WILL GAIN —

EARLY STAGES
OF CURING

LATER STAGES
OF CURING

179

H) FINISHING YOUR BOW : I DO NOT DO MUCH
SANDING ON A SINEW BACK. AT THE MOST, I
WILL TAKE A FLEXIBLE (SQUISHY) SANDING
BLOCK WITH 120 GRIT AND DO MINOR SANDING
BUT THAT IS ABOUT IT. AFTER SANDING I
DO WET THE BACK TO SMOOTH THE GLUE AND
SINEW.

AT THIS POINT, I WILL WRAP THE TIPS AND
HANDLE WITH SINEW. THE BOW IS NOT FINISH
TILLERED, BUT I WILL SMOOTH THE BELLY
AND SMOOTH ANY "STEPS" IN THE WOOD
FORMED BY FOLLOWING THE SCRIBE LINES.
TO KEEP SET BACK INTACT I DO SUGGEST
LEAVING THE HANDLE SECTION THICKER. I
SAND THE TIPS BY EYE AND YES, A BIT
OF GUESSWORK PRIOR TO TIP WRAPPING. IE,
AFTER TILLERING, THE TIPS ARE SLIGHTLY
THICKER THAN THE BELLY, IT ISN'T THE
END OF THE WORLD. LEARN AND APPL
LESSONS LEARNED ON FUTURE BOWS.

WRAP FROM NARROW TO WIDE - BY THAT, I
REFER TO BEGINNING YOUR WRAPS AT THE
NARROWEST POINT AND CONTINUE TOWARDS THE

180

✱ PRIOR TO ADDING WRAPS, SAND THE AREAS
OF THE BACKING WHICH WILL BE COVERED
AND SIZE THE SINEW AND THE BELLY WOOD.

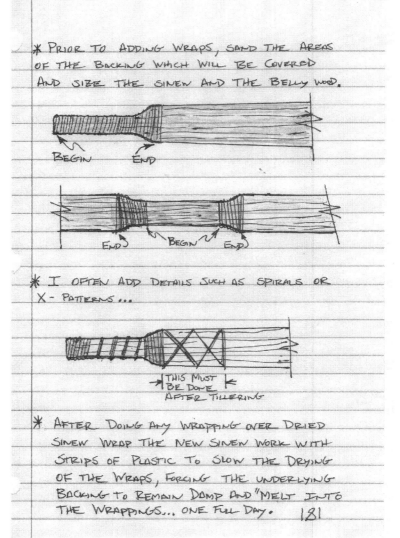

BEGIN   END

END   BEGIN   END

✱ I OFTEN ADD DETAILS SUCH AS SPIRALS OR
X - PATTERNS ...

THIS MUST
BE DONE
AFTER TILLERING

✱ AFTER DOING ANY WRAPPING OVER DRIED
SINEW WRAP THE NEW SINEW WORK WITH
STRIPS OF PLASTIC TO SLOW THE DRYING
OF THE WRAPS, FORCING THE UNDERLYING
BACKING TO REMAIN DAMP AND "MELT INTO
THE WRAPPINGS... ONE FULL DAY.   181

I) STRING GROOVES: I USE A 14 STRAND
B50 STRING WITH ONE LOOP, AND THE
OTHER END TIED ON. THE TIP OF THE
BOW AT THE LOOP END HAS TWO
GROOVES LIKE ANY OTHER BOW.

THE END THAT IS "TIED ON" WILL ONLY HAVE
ONE GROOVE. ONE GROOVE IS ALL THAT IS
NECESSARY WITH A   STRING ALONG WITH
BEING ACCURATE ON A NATIVE BOW.

THIS IS THE SIDE I GROOVE AS I AM RIGHT
HANDED AND TIE MY KNOTS ON THIS SIDE.

J) TILLERING: TILLER AS WOULD BE DONE
WITH ANY OTHER BOW — ALREADY COVERED, WITH
THE TILLERING STICK AND STRING. SPREAD
THE BEND OVER THE ENTIRE LIMB, AND
AIM FOR 45-50 POUNDS AT 17" MAXIMUM.

182

WHAT YOU MUST GUARD AGAINST IS THE FEELING THAT THESE BOWS ARE INDEST-RUCTIBLE — THEY ARE TOUGH AND CAN SUPPORT HIGH WEIGHTS, BUT OVERCONFIDENCE CAN KILL THEM. WITH A 50 INCH BOW, BRACED TO 4 INCHES, THEY COULD BE DRAWN TO 25 INCHES WITH CERTAIN WOODS (OSAGE) AND SUPPORT HIGH DRAW WEIGHTS. BUT, IN OTHER WOODS, DAMAGE COULD, AND MOST LIKELY OCCUR.... INSTANTLY. AIM FOR A MORE REASONABLE DRAW WEIGHT, AND BABY THEM WITH LOWER DRAW LENGTHS.....

"THEY PERFORM THEIR DUTIES
ON THEIR TERMS"

k) FINAL FINISHING CAN BE AS SIMPLE AS FINISH SANDING, GREASING, AND ADDING A SIMPLE HANDLE WRAP. IT CAN BE AS COMPLEX AS PAINTING, DYE PATTERNS, OR ADDING BEADS AND PORCUPINE QUILLS PLAITED INTO BANDS. IT IS YOUR BOW SO FOLLOW YOUR HEART. FOR WATER-PROOFING, I USE MINWAX'S ULTIMATE FLOOR FINISH: A WATER BASED POLY THAT WILL REMAIN FLEXIBLE.

183

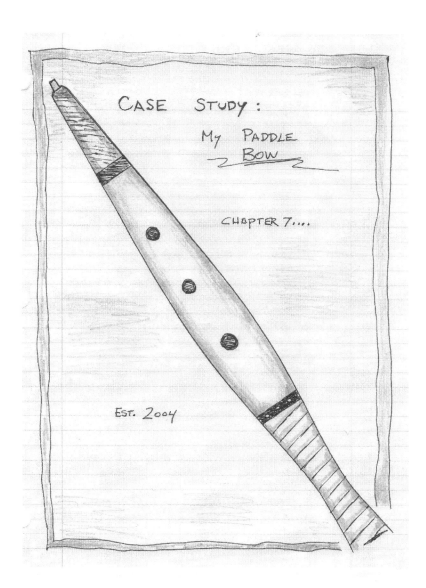

CASE STUDY:

MY PADDLE
BOW

CHAPTER 7....

EST. 2004

THE PADDLE BOW

UP UNTIL 2004, I WAS WHAT I
CONSIDER TO BE A HOBBYIST BOWYER.
YEP, I CONSISTENTLY MADE BOWS AND
EVEN SOLD A FEW HERE AND THERE...
BUT NO WHERE NEAR THE NUMBERS
THAT I MAKE NOW.

I'M NOT SURE WHICH MONTH IT WAS,
BUT IN 2004 I PICKED UP A COPY OF A
PRIMITIVE ARCHERY MAGAZINE AND IT
CHANGED MY LIFE. VOLUME 12, ISSUE
3 CONTAINED AN ARTICLE TITLED "THE
PADDLE BOW" WRITTEN BY A WELL
KNOWN BOW MAKER. THIS ARTICLE
NOT ONLY INTRODUCED THE PADDLE BOW,
IT ALSO INTRODUCED ME TO RED OAK
BOARDS AS A SOURCE OF BOW WOOD. UP
UNTIL THEN, MY SOURCES OF STAVES WERE
THE TREES I CUT; HICKORY, MAPLE, ELM,
WALNUT, etc., AND M BOWS WERE
SIMPLY D BOWS, BOTH SINEW BACKED
AND SELF, ALONG WITH THE TYPICAL
NARROW, DEEP HANDLED LONGBOWS.

READING THIS ARTICLE OPENED UP
A WHOLE NEW WORLD TO ME: RED
OAK PADDLE BOWS COULD GIVE ME
A WAY TO HELP SURVIVE THE STRUGGLE

To cover bills with the promise of developing a wonderful, reliable bow style using a consistant and easily obtained new form of bow wood.... So the work began.

My goal was to take what I learned from that article and not only develop my version of the paddle bow, but also figure out ways to build them efficienty enough to sell on this mysterious site called ebay. Up until then, my exposure to ebay was nonexistant, but there was a hope of digging my way out of debt, so I charged forward!!

Production bow building to me demands that, 1) the design must be developed in a way that will produce a great bow, and 2) the quality must be consistent. Red oak boards lend themselves to that. Well, between the time of reading that article and holding the first bow that I sold on ebay was measured in months, and since that time my bow has evolved into the form I build now.

185

I ESTIMATE THAT I HAVE SOLD
WELL OVER 200 PADDLE BOWS AND
CAN SAY THAT THERE ARE FOUR DISTINCT
EVOLUTIONS OF MY DESIGN. YES, THIS IS
A SPECIAL DESIGN FOR ME BECAUSE
IT REPRESENTS THE BEGINNING AND
THE FOUNDATION OF MY BOW MAKING
BUSINESS, IT IS MOST SPECIAL TO ME
BECAUSE IT IS A GREAT BOW....
IF I HAD TO MAKE A CHOICE OF WHAT
TYPE OF BOW I WOULD MAKE; I COULD
ONLY CHOOSE ONE, AND STICK WITH ONE
FOR THE REST OF MY LIFE, IT WOULD
BE MY RED OAK PADDLE BOW. I CAN
SAY WITH NO HESITATION, THAT I WOULD
BE HAPPY, ONLY MAKING PADDLE BOWS.

EVOLUTION #1 - MY ORIGINAL FACE SHAPE
    REMAINS TO THIS DAY. ALTHOUGH I DO
    VARY THE LENGTH FOR INDIVIDUAL
    BOWS, MY PADDLE BOW IS 66" LONG
    WITH THE WIDEST POINT ALONG THE
    LIMBS BEING 2½". AT THIS POINT I
    DID USE PIN NOCKS, BUT THEY WERENT
    AS DEVELOPED AS THEY ARE NOW.
    THE BACKS WERE BOARD LIKE, ONLY
    BEING ROUNDED ALONG THE EDGES.

186

EVOLUTION #2 - THESE BOWS VERY CLOSELY
RESEMBLE THE FIRST BOWS, BUT MY
HANDLES BECAME MORE ROUNDED, ALONG
WITH MOVING THE STRING GROOVES A
FULL INCH FROM THE TIPS UNLIKE 3/4"
IN THE FIRST BOWS.

EVOLUTION #3 - I BEGAN TO ROUND THE
BACKS AND SHAPE THE "FADES" TO
A GREATER DEGREE. I ALSO BEGAN
TO PAINT AND DYE THE BOWS. THESE
ARE BOW TYPES THAT I STILL
SELL, ALTHOUGH SOME OF MY BOWS
GO ALL THE WAY TO .....

EVOLUTION #4 - FULLY ROUNDING THE
BACKS. THESE BOWS HAVE NO FLAT
AREAS WHAT SO EVER ON THE BACK
WHICH DOES LIMIT ME TO ABOUT
50 POUNDS AT 28 INCHES, BUT
THEY ARE SO BEAUTIFUL. IF
YOU GO TO MY EBAY STORE,
JUANRIGGSARCHEY, THE HIGHLY PAINTED
BOW AT THE TOP OF THE PAGE IS
A GEN 4 BOW. THESE ARE RARE,
BUT I DO MAKE A FEW FROM TIME
TO TIME.

1) <u>TILLER</u> : IF YOU HAVE SEEN ONE
OF MY PB'S AT FULL DRAW,
EITHER ON A YOUTUBE
VIDEO OR FOR   SALE ON EBAY,
THIS IS THE SHAPE YOU WILL SEE.

THE BEND IS DISTRIBUTED EVENLY FROM
TIP TO HANDLE WITH NO STIFF AREAS
OR ANY OTHER ISSUES OF UNEVEN BEND.

THIS IS ONE OF THE KEYS OF MAKING A
64" NOCK TO NOCK, 50 POUND SELFBOW
THAT CAN HANDLE A 29" PLUS DRAW.
ANOTHER KEY IS TO TAKE THAT BEND
AND CREATE THE EFFECTS OF EVEN
STRETCHING ALONG THE BACK AND COMP-
RESSING ALONG THE BELLY, FORMING LONG
EVEN LINES OF STRESS.

THIS IS AN IMPORTANT CONCEPT : WITH
AN EVEN BEND RADIUS AND A LIMB THAT
GOES FROM NARROW TO WIDE, BACK TO
NARROWING TO THE TIPS, THE THICKNESS
PROFILE WILL NOT BE A CONSISTANT TAPER.

ALTHOUGH IT ISN'T SHOWN IN THIS SKETCH,
FROM THE HANDLE, THE LIMB THINS UNTIL
IT REACHES THE WIDE POINT ON THE

188

LIMBS, FOLLOWED BY A SLOW INCREASE IN
THICKNESS AS IT MOVES TOWARD THE TIPS.
UNLIKE MOST BOW WHICH HAVE A
CONSTENT TAPER, MY PADDLE BOWS
HAVE A DOUBLE TAPER WHICH IS
REVERSLY RELATED TO THE CHANGE IN
LIMB WIDTH. TO COMPLICATE MATTERS,
IT IS NOT A CONSTENT TAPER IN
EITHER DIRECTION OWING TO THE
CURVY SHAPE OF THE FACE PROFILE.
IT ALSO COMPLICATED THINGS OWING TO
THE DIFFERENCE IN LEVERAGE AT
DIFFERENT POINTS ALONG THE LIMBS.

2) WHY WIDE BOWS? FOR A GIVEN WEIGHT,
DRAW WEIGHT, A NARROW BOW WILL BE
THICKER THAN A WIDER BOW... MAKING IT
POSSIBLE FOR A WIDER BOW TO BE MADE
SHORTER, OR MORE COMPACT THAN THAT
NARROW BOW. IN EFFECT, A 2½" WIDE
BOW THAT PULLS 50 POUNDS IS LIKE
TAKING TWO 1¼" WIDE BOWS PULLING
25 POUNDS AND PLACING THEM SIDE
BY SIDE... SOMETHING TO THINK ABOUT.

A POSSIBLE DISADVANTAGE IS THE MASS
OF THE LIMBS. PB'S CURE THAT THROUGH
PROPER TAPERING AND HAVING LIGHT PIN

189

NOCKS. THE SPEED THAT I FIND WITH THESE CREATURES IS VERY GOOD WHEN THEY ARE COMPARED SIDE BY SIDE WITH A TYPICAL NON-RECURVED LONG BOW. I DON'T RUN THEM THROUGH A CHRONOGRAPH, BUT I DO FLIGHT SHOOT THEM WITH HUNTING WEIGHT ARROWS... AS SHOWN ON SEVERAL VIDEOS ON YOUTUBE, MY 60 POUND PB'S ARE CAPABLE OF 200 PLUS YARD FLIGHTS. THAT BY ANY STANDARD FOR A RED OAK SELF BOW IS VERY RESPECTABLE.

3) ALL IN ALL, IF A BOW IS BASED ON BEAUTY OF DESIGN, RELIABILITY, ABILITY TO WITHSTAND LONG STRING TIMES, AS WELL AS BEING GOOD PERFORMERS — THESE ARE GREAT BOWS AND HOW LUCKY I WAS WHEN I BOUGHT THAT PARTICULAR ISSUE OF THAT FINE MAGAZINE. PADDLE BOWS TAUGHT ME SO MUCH.

CHAPTER 8

THE BOWYERS FLOTE

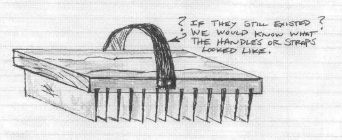

? IF THEY STILL EXISTED ?
WE WOULD KNOW WHAT
THE HANDLES OR STRAPS
LOOKED LIKE.

" OF WARBOW THINGS, BOTH
GREAT AND SMALL "

HERESY...

THERE HAPPENS TO BE A COAT OF ARMS BELONGING TO A BOW BUILDING SOCIETY THAT DATES BACK TO THE YEAR 1488. WHAT IS OF PARTICULAR IMPORTANCE OF THIS COAT OF ARMS IS THAT THERE IS A SINGLE TOOL SHOWN IN A PLACE OF HONOR UPON THE SHIELD, NOT ONCE, BUT IN THREE PLACES: THE BOWYERS FLOTE. A BOWYERS FLOTE IS COMPOSED OF MULTIPLE SCRAPING TOOLS, OR BLADES INSTALLED INTO A BLOCK, WITH A HAND STRAP, ALLOWING FOR A GREAT AMOUNT OF PRESSURE TO BE APPLIED TO THE STAVE.

I AM INTENTIONALLY BEING VAGUE IN NAMING THE GROUP WHO FLYS THIS COAT OF ARMS, ALONG WITH SKETCHING THE COAT OF ARMS ACCURATELY BECAUSE THE IMPORTANT POINT IS THAT THIS GROUP WAS INVOLVED IN THE MANUFACTURE OF LONGBOWS, AND I ASSUME WARBOWS DURING THE MIDDLE AGES.

WHY THIS IS IMPORTANT TO US IS THE MORPHING WE ARE GUILTY OF, OF VICTORIAN AGED "PROPER ENGLISH LONGBOWS" INTO OUR BELIEVED VISION OF A MUCH OLDER WARBOW OR LONGBOW. IT IS AN EASY LEAP TO TRACE THE ORIGIN OF THE BOW WE KNOW AS THE PROPER

191

ENGLISH LONGBOW: IT IS A DIRECT LINK TO
THE HIGHLY THOUGHT OF YEW LONGBOW. A MOST
BEAUTIFUL PARTNERSHIP OF MATERIAL AND DESIGN.
A POWERFUL WEAPON OF WAR THAT WAS OF
GREAT IMPORTANCE.

YEW, UNLIKE OTHER WOODS FAVORS THIS
NARROW, DEEP DESIGN WITH THE CHARACTERISTIC
ROUNDED BELLY.
UNLIKE ALMOST ALL
OTHER WOODS WHICH
CAN NOT DEFORM AND
THEN SPRING BACK, ALONG
THAT HIGHLY STRESSED
RIDGE, YEW IS ABLE TO COMPRESS
LIKE A COILED SPRING AND THEN REBOUND,
ALLOWING THE DEEPER BELLY WOOD TO SHARE
THE COMPRESSIONAL LOADS.

AREA OF
THE
GREATEST
COMPRESSION

OTHER WOODS SUCH AS ASH, ELM, OAK,
ETC. ARE NOT ABLE TO DO THIS AS WELL AS
YEW AND ARE FORCED BY THEIR COMPRESSIONAL
LIMITS INTO WIDER AND FLATTER CROSS
SECTIONS OR FACE MAJOR STRING FOLLOW OVER
TIME IF NOT OUTRIGHT FAILURE. * I HAVE
BUILT "ROUND BELLIES" IN THE PAST, BUT
EVEN THOUGH THEY MAY WORK WELL FOR A
PERIOD OF TIME, WITH CONSTANT USE, EVENTUALLY

192

THEY WILL SUFFER BECAUSE OF THEIR PHYSICAL LIMITS.

IN THE WORLD OF PROPER ENGLISH LONGBOWS, WE ARE LIMITED TO ONLY TWO MAJOR CHOICES FOR THE CONSTRUCTION OF A HEAVY BOW: A SELF BOW MADE OF YEW OR A TRILAMINATE OF "SUPER WOOD". BY "SUPER WOOD" I REFER TO THE LAMINATION OF TWO OR MORE WOODS WITH DIFFERENT CHARACTERISTICS – A PROCESS THAT WASN'T USED ON BOWS OF THE WAR BOW PERIOD. IN ADDITION, TRILAMINATE PROPER ENGLISH LONGBOWS ARE CONSTRUCTED OF WOODS NOT AVAILABLE IN OLD ENGLAND.

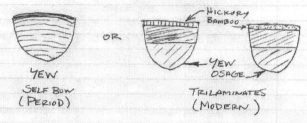

YEW
SELF BOW
(PERIOD)

OR

HICKORY
BAMBOO
YEW
OSAGE
TRILAMINATES
(MODERN)

IN MY SIMPLE MIND I ASK – IF WARBOWS WERE MADE FROM WOODS SUCH AS ASH OR WYCH ELM, AND THEY LOOKED LIKE WHAT WE ARE MADE TO BELIEVE: NARROW, DEEP, AND WITH ROUND BELLIES, JUST LIKE YEW BOWS, THEN WHY ARE OUR CHOICES IN MODERN TIMES EITHER YEW SELF BOWS

193

OR TRILAMINATES WHICH REQUIRE VARIETIES OF
WOODS NEVER USED BY MIDDLE AGES BOWYERS?

ONE ANSWER IS THAT THEY INTENTIONALLY
MADE INFERIOR BOWS OF WHITE WOODS BECAUSE
FORM WAS MORE IMPORTANT THAN FUNCTION.

ANOTHER ANSWER MAY BE THAT WIDER
BOWS WITH FLAT BELLIES ARE AN AMERICAN
INVENTION... AFTER ALL MANY PEOPLE CALL
FLAT BELLIED BOWS WITH NARROW DEEP HANDLES
"A. STYLE LONGBOWS". THAT FALLS APART REALLY
FAST BECAUSE BOWS SUCH AS THIS ARE ALSO
ANCIENT EUROPEAN DESIGNS; MEARE HEATH,
HOLMGAARD, MOLLEGABET, AND LATER, THE SAAMI
BOWS. EUROPEANS WERE BUILDING "A. STYLE LONG
BOWS" LONG BEFORE US, BUT ON BEHALF OF ALL
'MERICANS, THANK YOU FOR GIVING US THE CREDIT
FOR DOING SOMETHING RIGHT.

STILL ANOTHER ANSWER COULD HAVE BEEN
THAT THE BOW MAKERS OF OLD ENGLAND KNEW
HOW TO BUILD BOWS ACCORDING TO THE CAPABILITIES
OF INDIVIDUAL WOODS, BUT DARN IT, WE JUST
CHOOSE TO IGNORE THAT BECAUSE WE DON'T LIKE
THE WAY THEY LOOK. BUILDING TO THE WOOD IS
NOT A GROUND BREAKING REVELATION! ANYONE
WHO HAS SPENT ANY TIME BUILDING BOWS AND
IS ABLE TO LEARN FROM TRIAL AND ERROR, OR

194

LEARN VIA A LONG CHAIN OF OTHER BOW MAKERS
OVER A PERIOD OF HUNDREDS OF YEARS WILL
UNDERSTAND HOW DIFFERENT CROSS SECTIONS
ARE FAVORED BY DIFFERENT WOODS, TO
EFFECTIVELY PRODUCE HEAVY, FAST BOWS...

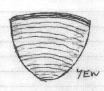

YEW

ASH, ELM, OAK, ETC.

    THIS IS BOW BUILDING 101 - IT IS
NOT IN ANY WAY ANY MORE MYSTERIOUS NOW
AS IT WOULD HAVE BEEN TO THE PROFESSIONAL
BOW MAKERS OF THE FAR OFF PAST.

    SOOO, YOU MAY BE ASKING, WHAT IS THE
IMPORTANCE OF THE BOWYERS FLOTE? WHY
WAS IT SO REVERED BY A WAR AND LONGBOW
GUILD THAT THEY FELT IT DESERVING TO
BE DISPLAYED ON THEIR COAT OF ARMS THREE
TIMES? WHY WAS IT SO CHERISHED THAT IT
WASN'T OVERTAKEN BY THE TOOLS USED TODAY
WHICH THEY HAD ACCESS TO? AND WHY IS
IT NOT BEING PRIZED TO THE SAME DEGREE
TODAY? HECK, IT HAS BEEN TOSSED ASIDE,
FORGOTTEN, BLOWN OFF....

195

BECAUSE IT HAS BEEN PROVEN OVER A LONG
PERIOD OF TIME THAT SOMETHING WITH THAT POWER
TO REMOVE MATERIAL IS NOT ONLY <u>NOT</u> NECESSARY TO
WORK YEW INTO BOWS, IT WOULD MOST LIKELY WORK
SOFT YEW TOO INTENSELY. THIS WOOD WORKING
BEAST HAS TO BE FOR WORKING TOUGHER WOODS
SUCH AS ASH, ELM, OAK, ETC INTO WIDER AND FLATTER
CROSS SECTIONS. IN EFFECT TO MAKE FASTER
PRODUCTION OF "MEAN WOOD" WARBOWS AND LONGBOWS
POSSIBLE. THE "MEAN WOODS" OR WHITE WOODS WERE
MORE AVAILABLE THEN YEW SO IT ONLY MAKES
SENSE THAT THESE BOWS WERE MADE IN GREAT
NUMBERS. "MEAN WOODS".... REMEMBER THAT.

YES, THIS IS HERESY TO SUGGEST THAT WHITE
WOOD WARBOWS (AND LONGBOWS) WERE FLAT BOWS,
OR TO BE LESS OF A HERETIC, FLATTISH BOWS.
BUT THERE HAS TO BE A POINT WHERE WE ASK
OURSELVES, "WHY WOULDN'T PEOPLE BUILD THE
BEST POSSIBLE BOW?" THAT ALONG WITH
BELIEVING THAT THE REVERED BOWYERS FLETE
SERVED A MUCH GREATER PURPOSE THAN A THING
TO FILL SPACE ON A SHIELD.

LEST I FORGET : COMPARED TO WORKING YEW
INTO A NARROW, ROUND BELLIED BOW, WORKING ELM
AND ASH INTO WIDER FLAT BELLIED BOWS WOULD
MAKE THESE WOODS SEEM MEAN. IT WOULD TAKE
A MEANER TOOL TO TAME THEM. THANK YOU
AND GOOD NIGHT.

33802899R00123

Printed in Great Britain
by Amazon